After
You Drop
Them Off

After
You Drop
Them Off

A Parent's Guide to Student Ministry

JERAMY CLARK
with Jerusha Ann Clark

Foreword by Wayne Rice

WATERBROOK
PRESS

AFTER YOU DROP THEM OFF
PUBLISHED BY WATERBROOK PRESS
2375 Telstar Drive, Suite 160
Colorado Springs, Colorado 80920
A division of Random House, Inc.

All Scripture quotations, unless otherwise indicated, are taken from the *Holy Bible, New International Version*®. NIV®. Copyright © 1973, 1978, 1984 by International Bible Society. Used by permission of Zondervan Publishing House. All rights reserved. Scripture quotations marked (KJV) are taken from the *King James Version*. Scripture quotations marked (MSG) are taken from *The Message.* Copyright © 1993, 1994, 1995, 1996, 2000, 2001, 2002. Used by permission of NavPress Publishing Group. Scripture quotations marked (NASB) are taken from the *New American Standard Bible*® (NASB). © Copyright The Lockman Foundation 1960, 1962, 1963, 1968, 1971, 1972, 1973, 1975, 1977, 1995. Used by permission. (www.lockman.org). Scripture quotations marked (NKJV) are taken from the *New King James Version.* Copyright © 1982 by Thomas Nelson, Inc. Used by permission. All rights reserved. Scripture quotations marked (NLT) are taken from the *Holy Bible, New Living Translation,* copyright © 1996. Used by permission of Tyndale House Publishers, Inc., Wheaton, Illinois 60189. All rights reserved.

Details in some anecdotes and stories have been changed to protect the identities of the persons involved.

ISBN 1-4000-7027-9

Library of Congress Cataloging-in-Publication Data
Clark, Jeramy.
After you drop them off : a parent's guide to student ministry / Jeramy Clark with Jerusha Ann Clark.—1st ed.
   p. cm.
 ISBN 1-4000-7027-9
 1. Church work with youth. I. Clark, Jerusha. II. Title.
BV4447.C515 2005
259'.23—dc22
                                                        2005007626

Printed in the United States of America
2005—First Edition

10 9 8 7 6 5 4 3 2 1

To Brian Aaby—
I can always count on you. No friend makes me laugh like you do
or consistently shows me what it means to be a youth pastor,
a husband, a father, and a man of God.

Contents

Foreword

One of the most encouraging trends in youth ministry today is what many people call family-based youth ministry. At its core is a long overdue appreciation of the important role parents play in the spiritual development of their teenagers, from their entry into the youth program through high school. That's why more and more church youth workers have been scrambling to devise new ways to reach out to parents, minister to them, and involve them in some way.

But as a wise person once said, "It takes two to tango." Despite our best intentions, family-based youth ministry just doesn't look very good when youth workers are the only ones who know the dance steps. We may be reaching out to parents, but they aren't always reaching back.

That's why I was so excited to read *After You Drop Them Off.* Veteran youth workers Jeramy and Jerusha Ann Clark have come up with the missing secret ingredient for successful family-based youth ministry. If you are a youth worker, you will want to put *After You Drop Them Off* in the hands of every parent you know. If you are a parent, you now hold in your hands an excellent guide for understanding, supporting, and interacting with the youth ministry of your church. This book gets everybody dancing to the same beat.

I have the opportunity to speak to thousands of parents every year, and I always encourage them to support their church's youth ministry. I usually say this more than once because I believe it's so important. Most parents nod their heads in agreement and write this bit of advice down in their seminar notebooks, but it's obvious from the anxious looks on their faces that they aren't exactly sure what I mean by this. Many of them probably interpret this admonishment in financial terms, as if what we're asking for is money to buy more water balloons and skateboard ramps.

Although money does help, what I mean is that parents and youth workers should treat one another as allies, not adversaries. There should be a relationship of cooperation, trust, and mutual respect that goes both ways between parents and those outrageous adults who have been called to work with teenagers and help them grow spiritually.

Parents, if your kids are involved in the youth ministry of your church, the first thing you should do is give thanks. Encourage them to stay involved. I know you might think some kind of reverse psychology is in play, and encouragement might cause them to stop going. Don't worry. This book will show you how to provide encouragement and support without throwing a monkey wrench in the gears.

If your kids are not involved in a youth group, read this book anyway. It will help you troubleshoot common problems. If you take an interest in youth ministry, there's a good chance your kids will too. If your church doesn't have a youth ministry, perhaps you can help start one. Or you may want to consider attending (or allowing your teenager to attend) another church that *does* have a thriving youth ministry. Now more than ever, teenagers can benefit greatly from being part of a youth group.

Maybe you aren't convinced. You may be thinking, *Well, I didn't go to a youth group, and I turned out okay.* Or *My kids are busy enough these days without adding one more thing to their schedules.* Or *I don't believe in forcing religion down my kid's throat. If he doesn't want to go, that's his decision.* You may have plenty of good reasons for not supporting your church's youth ministry, but consider the following points.

First, your kids need other adults involved in their lives besides you. While you will always be the most important adult presence in your children's lives, teenagers naturally gravitate toward other adults who will serve as mentors and role models for them. If they can't find actual real-life adults who they can access for free, they will likely settle for celebrities and other media substitutes. Youth groups usually surround kids with high-quality adults who love teenagers and are committed to their well-being.

Second, your kids need a network of friends, a community where they will be accepted, liked, and included. One goal of youth ministry is to provide quality relationships with peers and adults who care about them and share their faith and values. The engine that drives youth ministry is relationships.

Third, your kids need a place where they will be confronted and challenged with the truth of the Word of God and learn what it means to be a follower of Jesus in today's world. Sure, they hear it from you, mom and dad, but they also need to hear it from other adults and peers who express it differently and in a language they can understand.

Fourth, your kids need a safe place where they can ask tough questions, share their feelings, express their doubts, challenge traditions, and decide for themselves what their values and faith will be. They can't always do that at home or on their own. Effective youth ministries encourage and facilitate dialogue, exploration, experience, and discovery so that teenagers can get a fresh look at Jesus and make personal commitments that will last a lifetime.

Fifth, your kids need a place where they can participate in social activities that are fun without being illegal, immoral, or dangerous. Most youth workers today are experts at providing fun activities that kids love and parents don't have to worry (as much) about.

Sixth…well, I'll stop with five. The youth ministry you remember as a teenager has changed. It's no longer about keeping kids busy, entertained, and off the streets. Youth ministry now is about coming alongside and strengthening you and your family as the primary means of grace and nurture in the lives of your kids. You were never meant to parent alone, and youth workers were never meant to do youth ministry alone. While

today's youth workers are better trained and better outfitted than ever
before, they still need your support, encouragement, and, especially, your
prayers. This wonderful book will help you become the parent of every
youth worker's dreams.

—WAYNE RICE, cofounder of Youth Specialties and
director of Understanding Your Teenager seminars

Acknowledgments

Jerusha and I would like to acknowledge our thanks to…

Our Lord and Savior Jesus Christ—for the opportunity to write and for the gracious salvation in which we live and work every day.

Spence and Rona Clark—thanks for helping us become who God wants us to be. By the way, studying is *still* for nerds.

J.A.C. and LeAnn Redford—we love that our relationship is ever growing in strength and depth. And did you ever find out why a horse can't have a Social Security card?

Our Love Bug and Jazzy Jas—for the hugs and sloppy toddler kisses that keep us going.

Todd Hoyt—for a thousand and one breakfasts, and for being a great sounding board and excellent ministry partner. A-minus.

Doug Haag—one of the great fathers of youth ministry and a mentor whose wisdom continues to shape me.

Delores Thweatt—for giving your life to serve God, students, and families. Your insight and experience is invaluable to me.

Nancy and Brenda—for all your support and encouragement during the writing process. You ladies are a gift to our student ministries and the families involved in them.

Anjuli, Sam, Jenny, Dave, and Quincy—you are a true joy to work with, and I am grateful to partner with you in serving families. When should I take my vacation off the agenda?

To the faithful ladies in the weekday nursery: Janette, Janice, Kristy, Jackie, Jody, Kimie, Jen, Tomomi, Fumiko, Laurie, Claire—your loving care for Jocelyn and Jasmine has enriched their lives and, in many ways, made this book possible.

Richard and Marsha Williams—for being marriage mentors, ministry models, and simply amazing people.

Tom and Penny—for love and support that seems endless and easy at the same time. There's no one like UT and AP. We love you!

Kathy Hansen—for your prayers, for being willing to let our kids invade your home—*a lot!*—and for exemplifying joy in mourning. Your friendship is truly a gift from God.

Brittany—for (free!) baby-sitting when the editing *had* to be done and for loving our family with such sweet tenderness.

Steve and Don—for helping conceive this idea and for standing by us through four book projects.

Elisa—for your wise counsel in the proposal stage, your incisive line edit, and, most of all, your friendship. We cherish you and your family.

Shannon—for your keen and thorough editing skills.

Jennifer—for your meticulous attention to detail. This book is stronger as a result of your hard work.

The many parents who contributed their comments and shared their stories—you are a precious blessing to our life and ministry.

Becoming Allies

WHAT HAPPENS AFTER you drop your son or daughter off at church? Is youth ministry just a bunch of gross-out games and water wars, or is something deeper going on amid the loud music and frenzied activity?

I've worked with young people between the ages of eleven and thirty for fourteen years now. I've seen my share of "blender surprise" games, I've shaved my head in front of five hundred cheering students, and I've enjoyed some intense games of foosball, Nation ball, and laser tag. But activities like these are only a tiny part of what my ministry to students and their families involves.

Young people experience radical transformations once they enter adolescence. They change physically, emotionally, cognitively, relationally, and socially. They also begin to develop their own spirituality.

Research has shown that the majority of Christians begin a relationship with God before or during adolescence. Some research also indicates that after thirteen or fourteen years of age, the likelihood of conversion decreases significantly.

Rick Warren, pastor and author of *The Purpose-Driven Life,* observes that "junior high may be the single most pivotal period for spiritual decisions in the lives of our children."

As preteens and teens begin to think abstractly, they often reevaluate their childhood values. This opens the door for parents, pastors, and youth leaders to help young people establish a dynamic, personal relationship with Jesus Christ.

Perhaps you noticed that I include three groups of people as spiritual guides for students: parents, pastors, and youth leaders. I see these three groups as essential partners in directing the spiritual formation of young people. Peers also influence one another, but that's a topic for a different book.

While God charges parents with the primary responsibility of training their children in "the way [they] should go" (Proverbs 22:6), He also allows pastors and other leaders to come alongside families to equip and strengthen them for this exciting and terrifying task.

Sadly, parents and youth workers haven't always viewed one another as allies. Although in recent years most churches have emphasized the importance of ministry to students, when it comes right down to it, misperceptions and even fears about youth groups still plague many mothers and fathers.

Perhaps some parents participated in a student ministry when they were young and don't recall spiritual formation being a priority; fellowship and fun were the biggest concerns back then. Maybe some parents haven't been impressed with church youth leaders and their seemingly unprofessional dress, speech, and attitudes. Perhaps some parents wonder how a childless (let alone teenagerless) twenty-three-year-old could possibly have a spiritual impact on their sons or daughters.

This book seeks to dispel some of the myths about youth ministry and help parents and youth leaders avoid unnecessary conflict. I want to help bridge the gap and establish a vital partnership between parents and youth leaders. I hope this book will help unite parents and youth leaders, and I pray that lines of communication will be opened, that trust will be built, and that forgiveness and grace may be offered when necessary.

Doing this will require some changes in strategy and a commitment from both parties to invest time and energy in youth ministry. But I firmly believe that whatever we invest will yield amazing returns. As youth workers and parents join together with the common goal of ministering to students, extraordinary things can happen.

In this book I will investigate the purpose of youth ministry, what parents can expect from a student ministry, how parents can pray for a youth group, and how they can further the work with students at their churches. In doing so, I hope to equip parents with practical tools for partnering with the pastors and leaders who influence our children.

I also pray that I might offer some insight into how parents can constructively criticize student ministries and deal with disappointment. Finally, I would like to help parents think outside the youth-group "box" and eventually equip their kids for transitioning out of student ministry and into the "real world."

No matter how old your son or daughter is right now, what follows can help you form the relationships and collect the knowledge you need to maximize your child's youth-ministry experience.

The Importance of Family

In January 2004 twenty-two of the most influential youth-ministry leaders in the United States gathered to discuss the future of ministries to students and their families. After two days of prayer and dialogue, these leaders issued "A Call to Youth Ministers and the Church About Parent Ministry." They distributed this call to youth workers around the nation, asking them to sign the document as a declaration of agreement and support.

By signing the call, youth ministers admitted that "we as church and organizational leaders too long have failed to equip parents for their vital role in the spiritual instruction and leadership of their teenage children."

Youth leaders also agreed to "take on their rightful role as pastoral ministers to parents, acknowledging parents as the primary spiritual leaders of their children and serving parents in that role."[1]

In a similar fashion, I would like to issue a call to parents: Take on your rightful roles as prayer warriors for the student ministries at your church as well as enthusiastic supporters and faithful helpers of these ministries.

The entire church benefits from a strong youth ministry because the leaders of tomorrow are being trained in youth groups today. The whole family also profits from positive collaboration with a student ministry, since parents and youth workers complement one another and often provide what the other cannot. Many young people will listen to spiritual truth more readily from a discipleship-group leader than they will from mom or dad. Yet youth ministers cannot serve successfully without prayer support, encouragement, and understanding from parents.

The most effective way for youth workers to reach students is through the network of students' most important relationships: their families. I see a big part of my job as fortifying families so that sons and daughters might be more receptive to the truths of Christ that are lived out in their homes.

As parents, students, and youth leaders partner together, the world sees Christ through our love and unity. "The church makes its greatest impact upon unbelieving youth and families when its own youth and families are healthy spiritually."[2]

Getting Started

A few notes before we dig into the meat of this book.

First, you will notice that I often use such terms as "youth leaders," "youth ministers," or "youth workers" synonymously with "pastors and leaders." Some churches hire paid staff members to oversee student ministries. Others cannot or do not. Most youth groups, whether large or small, rely heavily on volunteer workers to run the programs, teach the Bible studies, and most important, love students. I use these terms interchangeably because I believe that parents can partner not only with paid staff members but also with the volunteers who impact their sons' or daughters' lives for Christ.

Second, you will note that at times I use the pronoun "he" when referring to a youth leader. The use of this pronoun is merely for the sake of convenience so that cumbersome language won't distract readers from the message of a particular chapter or paragraph. It's not my intention to show a preference for men as youth leaders, since both men and women have been charged by God to work with students. The majority of youth pastors in the United States are men, but many women also labor diligently in student ministries as youth directors or ministers, and they are often especially sensitive to the realities of working in a male-dominated field. So please bear with me as I use both the singular "he" and the inclusive "he or she" where these forms seem to fit best.

Now let's look at what God intends for ministry to students and their families as well as what parents can expect from a student ministry.

One

Purpose and Expectations

A CRISP OCTOBER wind picked up the last fallen leaves and tossed them around the church parking lot. I stood in the doorway watching, exhilarated by the sight of a steady stream of cars heading toward me. I knew the football game had let out and my night was just beginning.

No fewer than twenty sets of headlights lined up, waiting to turn left, while other Friday-night drivers wondered what was causing the backup. The cause of the traffic jam, our Friday-night coffeehouse, drew close to two hundred students, nearly half of whom came from unchurched families.

Higher Grounds, our student-run, adult-assisted coffeehouse, provided a place for nonbelievers to build relationships with Christians. Over the course of several weeks, we'd win a hearing through authentic relationship building and short testimonies. Early each winter we sponsored a lock-in event during which a speaker clearly presented the gospel. My youth team saw more than one hundred students dedicate their lives to Christ in the months before the lock-in as well as during the event.

Over the years I've seen few programs attract the number of unchurched students that Higher Grounds did. One Friday I shared Christ with a student who accepted the Lord and then began to plug into our weekly Bible study and Sunday services. I thought, *This is what ministry is all about!*

Yet on that blustery night in October, a relatively brief conversation revealed that not everybody agreed.

As Ethan, one of my core students, jogged to the door, he gave me a "What's up?" nod and trotted down the steps. His mom followed several steps behind, lost in a sea of chattering fifteen-year-old girls.

For this story to work, a note about our setup must be inserted here: Higher Grounds met in the basement of our church, and only one staircase led down to the action. I usually hung out in the doorway at the top of those steps for a while to both greet the students and act as crowd control. After most of the cars had unloaded, I'd head downstairs, and adult volunteers would make periodic rounds of the parking lot and other areas.

As Ethan's mom approached me, students continued to pour in through the doors. Without even pulling me out of the path of the incoming teenagers, she proceeded to tell me that she wasn't "a fan of the coffeehouse."

Her words didn't shock me. Other parents had expressed similar concerns, noting that building relationships with unbelievers could lead some students into temptation. I had always listened thoughtfully to these worries but encouraged parents to consider where else unsaved students could come to find Christ. Some kids who came on Friday nights wouldn't normally set foot inside a church, yet they felt safe at Higher Grounds. And not because we minced words about the good news. When our core students shared their testimonies, they proclaimed Jesus as the only way, truth, and life.

But back to the action that October night…

Ethan's mom began by telling me what she had heard through the grapevine. She asked me if I knew that there had been smoking, drinking, drug use, and sexual misconduct during Higher Grounds. Rumors such as these had been circulating among other anxious parents, so again, her words came as no surprise to me.

As she became more emphatic, students stopped to listen, and I felt uncomfortably aware that she and I stood at the only entrance to Higher Grounds. I finally pulled her aside, not only because I wanted some privacy, but also because I didn't want gossips spreading dirt about Ethan or his mom's concerns.

She seemed to feel frustrated that I did this, because her tone and conversation became increasingly dramatic. Completely exasperated after a few minutes, she finally said, "Well, my husband and I don't really see a need for a youth ministry anyway. There are no biblical grounds or model for it."

Nothing could have prepared me for her comment. I thought I could reassure her about the coffeehouse, but I wasn't prepared to defend the biblical grounds for youth work. I chose not to reply at that time and waited for her to continue. She didn't, so I thanked her and told her I would think about what she said.

And I *did* think about it. I kept thinking about it all night, especially as I watched Ethan. Not only was he a committed volunteer at the coffeehouse, but he also attended almost every event our group sponsored, including Sunday morning and evening services as well as Wednesday-night Bible study. As his core-group leader, I felt not only professionally but personally affronted by his mom's estimation of youth ministry.

Perhaps she wanted to ask me, "What's the point of the coffeehouse?" but instead she ended up asking, "What's the point of your job and your life work?" Maybe she wouldn't have summed up our conversation that way, but her final remark—"There are no biblical grounds or model" for youth ministry—left the most lasting impression on me.

Ethan's mom had never spoken with me before that night. She'd never volunteered at the coffeehouse or any other event, for that matter. She'd never asked me if she could visit on a Friday, Sunday, or Wednesday to see what we did. I could have dismissed her statements because of these facts. I could have concluded that she didn't know what she was talking about. But I didn't want to put our conversation out of my mind. Though I felt unsupported and even a bit angry, I needed to find the answer to her underlying question: What's the point of youth ministry?

In large part, this book grew out of my search for an answer to this question as well as my experience with parents—some like Ethan's mom and others who wholeheartedly support youth work. As a father myself, I know how concerned parents can be about the programs their children are involved in.

I *do* believe there are biblical grounds and models for youth work, and I feel that for biblical youth ministry to function well, youth leaders and parents need to share their wisdom and expectations with one another.

Maybe you, like Ethan's mom, have felt concerned that there doesn't seem to be a point to what goes on at church. Perhaps you've never met the youth leaders and feel out of the loop when it comes to their plans and vision for the youth ministry. Maybe you simply want to know what's going to happen and when. Perhaps you've longed to be involved in the ministry somehow, to pray for the students and leaders, or to share your resources with the group. If so, this book is for you!

Even as I write, I am reminding myself of what I'll need to know and do when my *own* girls enter our church's youth ministry. Join me now as we take a detailed look at what the Bible says about ministry.

WIN AND DISCIPLE: THE PROCESS OF PASSING ON GREAT TRUTHS

When Paul issued his final charges to Timothy, he stated, "The things which you have heard from me in the presence of many witnesses, entrust these to faithful men who will be able to teach others also" (2 Timothy 2:2, NASB).

Commenting on this verse, one well-known pastor writes,

As Paul directed Timothy in the process of transmitting the gospel message, he mentioned four generations of lives transformed by the grace of Christ. The first mentioned was his own generation....

The next generation was Timothy's. What he had heard, he was charged to deliver to others. These others would be the next generation.... These in turn would teach the next generation about "the grace that is in Christ Jesus." The process of spiritual reproduction, which began in the early church, is to continue until the Lord returns.[1]

The verse in 2 Timothy establishes a foundation for any ministry, including youth ministry. As a youth minister I feel somewhat like a Timothy. Older men of faith, such as my senior pastor, instruct me in the truths of Jesus Christ. Then I entrust what I have learned to the next generation "who will be able to teach others also." They are tomorrow's preachers and politicians, evangelists and electricians, missionaries and mothers.

Adolescents in America outnumber the populations of many world nations. Youth ministers go into the "foreign" countries inhabited by students and "make disciples of [these] nations, baptizing them in the name of the Father and the Son and the Holy Spirit." The Lord commands us to "teach these new disciples to obey all the commands I have given you" (Matthew 28:19-20, NLT). I intend to do that in my ministry to youth.

From this passage in Matthew, we see that the point of any ministry is twofold: to win converts and to disciple them. To win *students* to Christ and to teach them to obey what Jesus commanded—*this* is the purpose of *youth ministry*.

True, there are no specific references to "youth ministry" or "youth pastors" in the Bible. Only as the concept of adolescence gained acceptance did youth ministry begin. When much of the world began to view preteens and teenagers as a distinct group, separate from children and adults, the church responded by creating specific ministries to help students face the unique challenges they must deal with between the ages of eleven and eighteen.

For a young person who lives with nonbelieving parents, youth group can provide much-needed spiritual direction and training. For those privileged to enjoy Christian families, youth ministry reinforces what parents teach at home.

From the Bible we learn that youth ministry is part of the process of passing on the gospel to the next generation. This process begins with a student's commitment to Christ as Savior and Lord and continues with regular discipleship and spiritual formation.

No Christian parent I know would disagree with these goals. As moms and dads, we yearn for our children to know God and grow in faith, hope, and love.

Most simply, the Bible charges us to pass on what we've learned to the generations to come. This establishes the primary biblical grounds and responsibility for youth ministry. That is why youth pastors dedicate their lives to working with students. That is why I long to see families "get" what youth ministry is really about.

There Seems to Be a Point, but What About…

Most parents don't question, as Ethan's mom did, whether there's a point to youth ministry. Yet many wonder what *exactly* youth group is all about. As you may remember, Ethan's mom began by expressing her concerns about her son's safety and spiritual protection at a specific event. Only after her frustration escalated did she blurt out that she didn't see any biblical grounds for youth ministry.

Because actions speak louder than words, I don't believe that Ethan's mom disapproved of youth group altogether. If she really didn't see a point to youth ministry, she probably would have pulled her son from church activities. Even after our talk, she faithfully dropped him off for services and events. I think the deepest concern of her heart revolved around the unknowns of youth ministry—for example, "In going to the coffeehouse, would Ethan be influenced by 'bad company [that] corrupts good character'?" (1 Corinthians 15:33).

For parents who struggle to understand anything their preteen or teen does, youth group may seem like just another incomprehensible activity. They feel the tension between wanting to be involved enough to know what's happening and not wanting to alienate a child who feels that his or her space has been invaded.

Maybe you can identify with some of the concerns parents have shared with me over the years. For instance, have you ever wondered…

- What happens when I drop my son or daughter off at a youth event?
- What is my child studying or being exposed to?
- Who are the leaders who disciple my child?
- How can I partner with the youth ministry without freaking out my child?
- How can I approach the leaders of my son's or daughter's youth group with my concerns?
- How can I pray effectively for the youth ministry?
- How can I help the youth ministry if I don't have enough time to volunteer regularly?
- How can I deal with my child's (or my own) disappointment with a church's youth ministry?
- How can I prepare my son or daughter to leave youth ministry after high-school graduation and stay connected to the church?

Whether or not you've actually voiced these questions, maybe they have helped you pinpoint somewhat nebulous feelings you've had about youth group.

There's no guarantee that after reading this book you'll be convinced that youth ministry is an essential part of the church body, but I plan to do my best to persuade you that many students *and families* can benefit from a church's youth program.

I also hope this book fills a void for parents, like Ethan's mom, who long to understand youth ministry. Even Doug Fields, *Purpose-Driven Youth Ministry* guru, recognizes that "there are very few models, resources, and practical ideas on how to minister to both parents *and* students." Though many youth pastors desire to minister to youth *and* their families, "the youth ministry world…has been slow to show us the practical side of this new paradigm."[2]

This book aims at practicality and includes many tips and tools for parents who want to make the most of their child's church experience by partnering with a youth ministry. After you've read it, I hope you'll feel equipped to do your part in creating a healthy partnership between your family and the youth pastors, directors, and volunteers who work with your children. Like me, most of them probably desire to join with you in training up your sons and daughters in Jesus Christ.

WHAT DO YOU EXPECT?

The verb *to expect* can bring to mind these definitions: "to look forward to with anticipation" or "to consider something reasonable and due." The definition you choose to live by determines much of your attitude toward life. Either you look forward to what might come or you consider the things you want as your "reasonable" right.

All parents approach youth ministry with specific expectations. Some hope for the best, look for the positive, and anticipate that a youth program will benefit their son or daughter. Others await the fulfillment of their agenda and purpose for the youth group, supposing that things should happen in a certain manner and time—namely, *their* manner and time.

Over the years of working with youth and their families, I've encountered parents along the entire spectrum, ranging from supportively expecting to utterly demanding. Through parent meetings and letters home, our ministry seeks to communicate a clear purpose and vision for the youth group, but it's difficult to address or change a person's expectations without personal dialogue.

That's why I'd like to explore expectations before jumping into the rest of the book. Here's a quick overview of a few of the expectations parents have articulated to me over the years. Perhaps a few of these sum up your hopes as well. For some, youth ministry is…

- an adolescent day care; a teen-sitting service, if you will
- a program designed to keep their kids entertained and happy
- an opportunity for their child to be "saved"
- a place that supports parents' biblical instruction
- an opportunity for discipleship and fellowship for their child

Let's look more closely at each of these expectations and identify their good and bad aspects. While my evaluation of a student ministry's goals may not represent *every* youth group, I hope it will clue you in to what a majority of youth workers pray that parents might expect.

"Just Watch My Child for a While"

The expectation that a youth ministry provide adolescent baby-sitting is not *altogether* flawed. But since you've picked up a book on youth ministry, I'd guess this isn't your main expectation.

Even so, it's perfectly normal and healthy for parents to want some time away from their teens. The challenges of raising children between eleven and eighteen years of age can be exhausting. A midweek or weekend rest for a tired mom and dad can be a good thing, indeed.

The trouble comes when parents have no *greater* hope than this for a youth ministry. When parents view youth group only as a teen-sitting service, they're unlikely to support the ministry or volunteer to help.

Sadly, I've seen parents who barely slow down to let their child out of the car! They don't care what's happening at an event (it has to be something wholesome if it's at the church, doesn't it?) as long as it keeps their son or daughter occupied for a few hours.

If you or your spouse has felt this way, it might benefit you to make an appointment with the youth staff members and find out what their ministry is really about. If you catch a vision for where they're headed over the next few years of your teen's involvement in youth group, you may find yourself raising the bar of your expectations.

Perhaps you don't see youth ministry as a teen-sitting service, but you know of a family that does. If you've developed a relationship with that family, you could consider speaking with them gently but specifically about what happens when they leave their child at church.

"Just Keep My Child Happy"

Some parents simply want their child to be entertained at church. They want a positive version of MTV—music, real-life stories, and wild games. They're satisfied if they see a calendar loaded with events, especially during the summer when their child is out of school and could easily become bored or get into trouble.

This expectation comes with the hope that youth ministry will keep a student happy. Families may anticipate that youth group will keep students away from destructive influences and/or ensure that they don't fall into depression, rebellion, or any number of negative behavioral patterns.

While there's nothing wrong with desiring your child's happiness and well-being, youth ministry cannot prevent a student from making poor choices or from being sad. Many eleven- to eighteen-year-olds suffer through periods when their bodies and emotions are changing so rapidly that nothing seems to make them happy. As youth leaders, we, too, long for your child to be fulfilled, to make wise decisions, and to experience joy in the Lord. We want to see your son or daughter grow and find peace during tumultuous times in his or her life. Most youth staffers desire to come alongside you and help in whatever way they can to develop Christ-likeness in your child.

But youth ministry cannot make a student happy. It can merely help a student find happiness and enjoyment in certain things, such as Bible study, fellowship, events, and most significantly, the Lord Jesus.

"Save My Child, Please!"

Recently I received a phone call from a desperate parent of one of my current students. His son had become involved in some activities that were not pleasing to his parents or to the Lord. The dad didn't give me details of his son's spiritual state, but I sensed from the tone in his voice that he ached for his child to find or return to the Lord.

After a few minutes of conversation, I offered to pray with this father. But when I closed my prayer, the dad asked when he thought his son might be saved. I told him I didn't know and suggested that he continue asking the Lord to bring his son to repentance.

He sounded a little frustrated as he countered, "Well, what are *you* going to do?" I tried to reassure him that prayer was not only the best weapon for both of us but also the only real weapon. I offered to try to find a mentor for his son or meet with him myself. But I added that there wasn't much else I could do if his son had no interest in me or the church.

Incensed, he said, "But isn't it your job to save my son?"

I wish I could have told this dad when his son would be saved. Not only couldn't I tell him that I could save his son, I didn't even want to tell him I'd *attempt* to save his son. Only God can save. I believe deep down this father knew that, but like many parents, he held unrealistic expectations of youth ministers.

My job—the job of any youth pastor or leader—is not to save students. Rather, in God's strength, youth ministers can shepherd by His grace, pray with His power, and faithfully preach the good news in season and out (see 2 Timothy 4:2). By His grace, God may use me or someone else to impact a student's life.

Once again, some of the desires that undergird this expectation are noble ones. All godly parents want to raise godly children. But a student ministry can only help so much. A mom or dad can only do so much. God is the One who woos, reveals the truth, convicts of sin, and ultimately saves.

"Help Me Teach My Child"

Parents who invest time in their son's or daughter's spiritual growth often approach me and request that I back them up by supporting what they teach at home. Indeed, this expectation for youth ministry is far more positive than negative. A youth ministry can shore up what godly families learn together. It can confirm the truths of Scripture, affirm the character of God, offer opportunities for commitment to God, present chances to repent from sin, and provide times for authentic interaction with other believers.

As I mentioned earlier, in the last decade or so, authors and speakers like Doug Fields, Jim Burns, and Josh McDowell have encouraged youth pastors to view their job as a ministry to students *and* their families. This paradigm shift has gone a long way to open channels of communication between parents and youth pastors who can work together as a team to teach students biblical perspectives.

I recall one volunteer leader who approached me and asked if he could take his group of sophomore guys through a study of creationism and biblical views of physical science. At school these young men were being taught evolution and other theories as if they were fact. This leader wanted to help his students discover the truth for themselves and learn how to defend their faith with solid, logical reasoning. I wholeheartedly encouraged him to start that study and to continue finding connecting points with his students outside of church. I know the parents of these young men appreciated this leader's attentiveness to what his group was being taught at school.

There can, however, be negative aspects to this "work with me" expectation. Parents have sometimes insisted, for instance, that our youth ministry teach a particular view about gray areas in Scripture (such as dating) or doctrines of the faith (such as eschatology), issues about which great men of God on both sides hold equally defensible views.

Parents have also asked that I tailor our youth-group studies to a specific topic or book of the Bible that they are examining at home. I always consider their request, but realistically I cannot alter the church's entire program based on what one family is doing during their devotional time. If, however, a suggestion reveals a widespread need in our group, I'll do what I can to teach accordingly.

For example, the high-schoolers I worked with in Colorado struggled with cliquishness and exclusivity. Some parents who had assessed the situation over time encouraged me to speak to this issue. I agreed with their observations and challenged the students to reach out of their tightly knit groups. What a great partnership with families that was!

If you would like to meet with your child's youth pastor or leader about supporting what you teach at home, keep in mind that other students in the group may be studying something different with their families. Ask God to help you make articulate suggestions, not demands. He will enable you to speak graciously when you ask Him to do so.

A youth worker may not be able to incorporate all that you're teaching at home, but you can always take what is being taught at youth group and dig deeper into those scriptures during your family devotions.

"Help My Child Grow Spiritually and Have Fellowship"

I take very seriously Christ's command to disciple students. Again and again in the Bible, Jesus called undershepherds to feed the sheep (see John 21:17) or, in clearer terms, to instruct people in the truth. I consider responding to this challenge a nonnegotiable for all youth pastors. For this reason I also expect a youth ministry to connect each student with an opportunity to be discipled.

Since we have a large number of students in our youth group, I seek volunteer leaders who can meet weekly—or more often, depending on their availability—and disciple a small group of students. I like to keep the number of students in our core groups to between six and eight, but group size can fluctuate as students come and go.

By no means is this the only model for encouraging discipleship and spiritual formation, but it is one I have found effective. Even in youth ministries with no official small-group structure, leaders or parents can initiate Bible studies or fellowship groups. (By the way, this may be something you'd like to do if your child feels lost in the crowd at church—even if that crowd is only twenty students! I'll give you some hints on how to start such a group later in the book.)

Most youth leaders also consider fellowship a high priority for their ministries. In Acts 2:42, the early church is described as "continu[ing] steadfastly in the apostles' doctrine and fellowship" (NKJV).

Some churches think candle parties and potlucks fill the fellowship quotient. While socializing is certainly a crucial aspect of authentic community, fellowship cannot be limited to events, activities, or opportunities to hang out with others. Biblical fellowship includes bearing one another's burdens, committing to pray for and help one another, and being real with others so that they can provide encouragement and accountability.

The biblical charge to fellowship with other believers led me to connect students with a small group. Real fellowship cannot happen only in large groups or over doughnuts and lattes. Authentic communion with other believers occurs as students both give and receive, entwining their lives with one another in God.

Many youth ministries have moved toward a small-group structure. These groups may be called by a host of names, such as cell groups, D (for discipleship) groups, fellowship groups, or, as we call them, core groups. Most of these groups foster both life-on-life instruction in the truth as well as life-to-life fellowship.

If your youth group is small enough to offer both discipleship and fellowship to *all* the students, the group may not need to be broken down further. Sometimes, however, even within a small ministry, it helps to have separate accountability groups for the young men and women.

Should you sense that your child has not connected with a small enough group to experience both discipleship and fellowship, talk to the youth pastor about options available at your church. If none of his suggestions work, look for other opportunities for your son or daughter to have fellowship and be discipled. He or she could attend the meetings of an organization such as Student Venture. Or your child could get involved with a Christian club or a Fellowship of Christian Athletes Huddle. (Groups like these will be discussed in greater detail in chapter 9.)

Parents can view these organizations as youth ministries as well. I'll explore this idea later in the book, but for now, let me assure you that most of these associations share the same goals and priorities as churches. Just make sure your child understands that these organizations are intended to complement the church, not replace it. Consider it a warning sign when a student wants *only* to connect with such groups.

The only negative aspect of this discipleship-and-fellowship expectation is that parents sometimes assume that their child will *want* to be discipled and participate in fellowship. The sad reality is that some students are not interested in such commitments. If a student feels this way, I do what I can to encourage connection with others and foster a desire for discipleship. But I can only do so much. *Any* youth pastor can only do so much. A student must decide for him- or herself whether to give a small group a chance.

What Parents Like You Had to Say

At the end of each chapter in this book, you will find "real-life" comments from parents who have healthy expectations for youth ministry. I hope these will encourage you to develop your own balanced view of what a youth ministry can offer your child.

From Rich, a father of three, one in high school, one in junior high, and one in elementary school:

> I come from a somewhat different perspective than many average families. My kids are homeschooled. My wife and I hope to integrate all of our family's goals with a student ministry. I've seen some parents use youth group as what I'd call a "crutch"; they want the ministry to raise their kids spiritually. I would simply like to see a ministry provide opportunities for the development of spiritual gifts and leadership abilities. My kids having a good time is a bonus. Out of the relationships they make at church will come the fun and joy that the Lord designed relationships to provide.

From Janice, mother of two boys, one in junior high and one in high school:

> What I look for in a youth ministry is that it does not concern itself merely with social activities. My first priority as a parent is to biblically train up my sons, and I would like a youth group to support that endeavor, complementing what I teach at home. I expect information to be available for special events as well as

regular activities. When it comes to my son's spiritual development, the last thing I want is to be thrown a curve ball!

From Kathy, mother of six, who has had at least three students in a youth ministry at any given time over the past decade:

I expect a youth group to be biblically based. I also feel a group should have a balance of fun and serious activities. A ministry should definitely encourage discipleship. For me, a commitment to support the needs of families, sensitivity to the financial needs of parents with more than one child involved, and a respect for family time are also important. I don't want my kids out of the house every night of the week. Finally, it's essential that good boundaries for behavior be established and that adult leaders be appropriately involved in my students' lives.

Two

What's Happening?

WHEN GRETCHEN AND her family started attending a new church that billed itself as "seeker friendly," she had some reservations about her son's participation in the youth ministry. The meat of God's Word and a commitment to discipleship sometimes seemed to be lost amid events and sermons targeted at the unsaved. Too often for Gretchen's liking, Tyler came home and told her that he hadn't even opened his Bible during Sunday service.

Furthermore, the youth ministry at Gretchen's church was a combo junior-high and high-school group, so seventh-grade Tyler and the other twelve-year-olds had been thrown together with guys who could grow full beards and girls who had been shaving their legs since Tyler was in kindergarten.

When she picked Tyler up from midweek programs, Gretchen noticed that things appeared a bit out of control or, at the very least, disorganized. Gretchen tried to give the youth staff the benefit of doubt—"It's probably just like that when an event is wrapping up," she rationalized—but deep down she felt that something was amiss.

One night Gretchen decided to pick her son up from church early. Though she expected some cheesy heart decorations and sappy music at the youth group's Valentine's Day event that night, she didn't anticipate finding Tyler in a dark room where students were slow dancing to the secular song "Rock Your Body."

I'm *not* joking! This happened when Tyler, now a senior in high school, was a junior-high student.

While Gretchen felt it essential that her son have a place to bring his non-Christian friends where they could hear the gospel, she did *not* feel that nonbelievers could encounter Christ at a dance like this. More likely, students were meeting others who they hoped were boyfriend or girlfriend material. At least that's what it looked like. Inappropriate touching seemed to be going on all over the place, even between students and leaders. Horrified, Gretchen watched one teenage girl throw her arms around a twentysomething male leader in a tight embrace.

Gretchen wanted to kick herself. She had been leery of allowing Tyler to go to the Valentine's event since no information had been provided beforehand. But the mood lighting and sensuous music felt like a curve ball hitting her right between the eyes. She had no idea the group would follow the world's model to this extent.

Collecting herself so as not to appear frantic, she found Tyler and led him out of the building. She asked him some questions on the way home and discovered that he had spent most of the evening playing foosball with a couple of guys he knew from school. Though Gretchen felt this might not have been the most profitable use of his time, at least he wasn't trying to rock anyone's body.

Needless to say, Gretchen and her husband had a talk when she got home. They left the church shortly thereafter and found a church that had a commitment to discipleship, a respect for the Word of God, and a healthy approach to winning the lost to Christ. She and her husband became involved with the youth ministry at this new church so that they would know what went on from week to week. They both found they enjoyed working with students, and they stayed on as small-group leaders.

Perhaps you haven't had a shell-shocking experience like Gretchen had. For many parents (like me!), this resembles one of their worst nightmares. Removing myself from the role of youth pastor and just speaking as the father of two daughters, I don't know that I would have remained as composed as Gretchen. I would have wanted to have a little talk with whoever thought this Valentine's Day dance was a good idea.

Or maybe you've been thrown by something that happened—or didn't happen—at church. Some parents don't realize, for instance, that certain events have different purposes: some are for spiritual growth, some are for outreach, and some are for fellowship. If parents expect every church activity to follow the same pattern, they may feel disappointed or confused when events don't look quite the way they anticipated.

You may be reading this and thinking, *I have no idea what happens when I drop my child off at church. What if she's sitting on some leader's lap? What have I been thinking? I need to find out what is going on at our church ASAP.*

Wherever you're at right now, don't despair! This chapter will give you a glimpse into what happens at a typical youth ministry event. Of course my experiences and models represent a particular way of running a ministry that may not be shared by everyone. Even so, I pray that this chapter will offer you a general idea of what might be happening at your church.

THE FIRST LOOK

As I mentioned in the previous chapter, many youth ministries divide students into small groups. Within these smaller core groups, young men and women receive care they might miss in a larger group. Large-group events can be important for building relationships and providing opportunities for nonbelievers to encounter Christ, but without a more intimate place for discipleship, students tend to fall through the cracks.

I am a huge fan of small groups for a number of reasons, but I'd like to highlight just a few of the main reasons.

1. In core groups, adult leaders become shepherds rather than a police force. They don't merely chaperon; they provide much-needed guidance. Paul exhorted others to "follow my example, as I follow the example of Christ" (1 Corinthians 11:1). In the same manner, adult volunteers and youth staff members encourage young men and women to model their lives after the Lord as well as the godly mentors He's placed in their lives.

2. A ministry's "back door" shrinks when churches utilize a small-group structure. We youth pastors use the phrase *back door* to refer to the proverbial point at which students leave a ministry. Inevitably, we lose some kids to other activities, the pressures of life, even other youth groups. But if students feel that their needs are being met in a group, they find it less desirable to miss core-group time, let alone ditch a youth ministry altogether.

3. Students cannot hide in core groups. Even in a small crowd, quiet or embarrassed students can "disappear." Students who are living in disobedience can avoid accountability, and those harboring deep hurts can miss the chance to find healing and support.

   In an ideal world, every student would be connected to other believers—in a large or small group—in such a way that they would not only grow in intimacy with God and one another, but they would also feel safe to be themselves. In a situation like this, students would be free to express their feelings as well as to ask for prayer and help.

4. Small groups can reveal God's love for students in powerful ways. But that can only happen when leaders share both the gospel and *their lives* with students. In 1 Thessalonians 2:8,

Paul told the church that he and his co-laborers invested in individual lives, not simply in large groups. "We loved you so much," he wrote, "that we were delighted to share with you not only the gospel of God but our lives as well, because you had become so dear to us." Young people may not recall what their pastor preached a month ago, but they will likely remember when their youth leader prayed for them before a big event or comforted them when they were hurting.

If your church has a small-group structure, these characteristics may already be part of your child's youth ministry. Core groups can form the foundation for a ministry that connects students in life-on-life, spiritually forming relationships.

At this point you may be thinking, *I don't know if there are small groups at our church.* Or perhaps, *I've seen what goes on in the youth ministry at my church, and this doesn't describe it at all.*

I can offer two bits of advice to those who feel like this:

First, don't assume that just because your church doesn't have a small-group format, genuine discipleship and growth are not happening. Find out for yourself what is actually going on. (I'll give you some tips for how to do this later in the chapter.) If after checking things out yourself, you discover that the youth ministry at your church has no real commitment to spiritual development, consider helping your child find a place where he or she *can* be nurtured.

Second, remember that small-group ministry is just one way to disciple students. There are other ways in which pastors can come alongside parents to train young people in godliness. Smaller churches may prefer one-on-one mentoring or staying together during worship and study times. Again, find out firsthand what is going on in your son's or daughter's youth group, and determine whether this is the best way to meet his or her spiritual and relational needs.

Doing Your Homework

Your child probably does a fair amount of homework daily. You may be relieved that you don't have to suffer through geometry proofs or biology tests anymore, but let me encourage you to do a little homework of your own to find out specifics about the youth ministry your son or daughter attends.

While working in Colorado, Jerusha and I developed a relationship with a neat homeschooling family. They had us over for dinner (fantastic grilled burgers, if memory serves) and truly wanted to get to know our family outside of a ministry context.

Now I have to tell you this cool aside: Greg, the father, made a living building gorgeous cabinetry. When I first arrived at the church, he offered to install some cabinets in my church office. I thought they'd be nice enough, but nothing could have prepared me for the awesome hand-crafted cabinets—complete with crown molding—that his assistant put up in my office.

The family-ministries pastor, who still had particle-board-and-cinderblock shelves, asked me how I, the fresh-faced youth guy, got so lucky. Even the senior pastor didn't have cabinets as nice as mine.

This aside about the cabinets actually has a point: Greg and his wife went out of their way to connect with me and bless me. Greg also asked if he and I could meet now and then.

Over coffee and skillet meals at the smoky Village Inn near our church, we discussed philosophies of ministry, teaching plans, how trips were handled, who on my staff shouldered which responsibilities, and so on.

I remember those times fondly, though Greg and I didn't always see eye to eye. We respected each other as Christian men committed to raising tomorrow's leaders, and I always went away refreshed by our times together.

It didn't surprise me that when I introduced a series on relationships in our youth group, Greg asked if he could sit in and hear my perspective. At the time Jerusha and I were writing our first book on the subject—*I Gave Dating a Chance.* The book had not been published yet, so Greg didn't know where we stood on the issue. Like many godly parents, Greg wanted to monitor what his fourteen-year-old daughter, Angela, heard about relationships with the opposite sex. He was concerned that she might be exposed to ideas that weren't appropriate for her stage of life or that weren't in line with his family's philosophy.

His desire to participate in the discussion about relationships fit right in with what Jerusha and I encouraged in *I Gave Dating a Chance* and continued to emphasize in our second and third books on the subject. In all three works we exhort parents to read our books before or with their child, using the chapters and study questions as a springboard for conversation and to help forge a shared vision on crucial relationship topics.

In a nutshell, these were the goals I presented to our youth group for my series on relationships: (1) I wanted to help students place in a proper biblical perspective any feelings they might be having for members of the opposite sex; and (2) I wanted students to consider these godly options: not dating, courting, or focused dating. I never endorsed dating as the best way. I simply exhorted students to make an informed choice based on their parents' will and God's standards.

Greg and his wife had decided that they would not allow their children to date, and they didn't want Angela, a freshman at the time, to question her parents' authority. During the series, Greg pulled his daughter out of the youth group.

Greg and I parted ways with mutual respect. We merely disagreed on whether dating, as an institution, was inherently flawed. I affirmed his decision to withdraw Angela from the group and esteemed him for hold-ing firmly to the commitments he and his wife had made.

Greg did his homework and determined that his daughter shouldn't hear a particular set of teachings. Other series and sermons of mine had been "right on" in his estimation, but he felt uncomfortable with my teaching on this topic. Greg would never have known, however, what his daughter was hearing if he hadn't investigated the matter himself.

Now let me share a story about the relationship series that ended differently.

Jill and her daughter had always had a close relationship. When Rachel entered her freshman year of high school, Jill started working as a core-group leader for some senior girls. She knew that Rachel's core-group leader in junior high had had a positive impact on her daughter, and Jill wanted to disciple some young women herself.

Jill also longed to spend more time with Rachel, who was becoming increasingly busy with school and church activities, and she wanted to find out firsthand what was going on in the youth group. She had visited the junior-high ministry a couple of times and felt that she'd gotten the pulse of that group. Now that Rachel was going to be involved in a high-school group for four years, Jill wanted more than a cursory knowledge of what happened week to week.

As Greg had done, Jill approached me and asked what my series on dating would include. She felt it would be a good idea to allow Rachel to hear what I presented, but she wasn't sure Rachel was ready for or even interested in these ideas.

After the first two weeks of teaching, however, it became apparent to Jill that not only was Rachel concerned about relationships, but she also needed guidance in applying the scriptures and ideas my sermons introduced.

Jill told me later that the series allowed her to see a different side of her daughter, a side Rachel had been leery of sharing with her mother before hearing the talks. My teaching afforded Jill and Rachel an opportunity to discuss their family's position on dating as well as God's wisdom on the subject. My talks jump-started communication between mother and daughter on a significant issue, and that is exactly what I hope to accomplish by preaching to and serving families.

Again, Jill would have missed this chance if she had not done her homework and discovered what Rachel studied at church from week to week.

I've Observed...

Working at the First Evangelical Free Church of Fullerton as a lead associate youth pastor with a group of five hundred students and now pastoring my own youth ministry of three hundred plus students at Emmanuel Faith Community Church (EFCC), I've seen many parents drop in periodically during various youth events to either check out what is happening or to hear teaching on a certain subject. Many moms and dads also stop by to connect with me, a core-group leader, or another staff person. Parents sometimes participate in weekly youth activities as well, which I find encourages their son's or daughter's spiritual growth.

Many Sunday mornings at both First EV Free and EFCC, parents sit in the back or on the sides of the youth room, joining in the service and providing a much-needed example to students, many of whom will become parents someday.

When my wife, Jerusha, was in high school, her parents dropped in occasionally on her youth group simply because they enjoyed the energy and spirit of high-school worship. I've known other parents who've done the same.

Parents stop by less frequently on Wednesday nights during the school year since we devote a good 75 percent of our time together to small-group activities. But I do sometimes meet with parents during that time.

I notice more moms and dads coming during special events or summertime activities when we take a break from core-group structure. Some parents offer to drive as a way to connect with the students and leaders in our ministry; others volunteer to help with setup or cleanup at barbecues and other events.

Last summer a concerned mom and dad asked me if they could come to Wednesday nights throughout the summer. At that time our ministry met "off campus" (translated, away from the church). A wonderful family hosted us, offering their pool, grill, basketball courts, and expansive lawn for our worship and teaching time.

These concerned parents could easily blend into the crowd of students and adults gathered on Wednesday nights. They were glad for that. You see, these parents had a specific purpose for attending our midweek events. Their seventeen-year-old daughter had recently started dating a young man, and they felt anxious about some inappropriate behaviors they'd noticed. They wanted to observe the couple from afar to see how the two interacted at church.

I still don't know if this girl realized that her parents came to youth group throughout the summer. But I saw this mom and dad week after week and assured them that my job was to support the entire family, not defend their daughter or take her side because I was her pastor. My ministry is to families, and I want to aid parents in any way I can as they train up godly children.

A more humorous thing happened to me and a large group of parents who wanted to hear me preach during my first year at Emmanuel Faith Community Church. I had been serving at EFCC for around six months when I discovered that the church had a tradition of inviting moms to the youth service on Mother's Day.

My staff and I began planning the morning a couple of months in advance. As my team brainstormed, someone suggested asking our senior pastor's wife to teach. Though a celebrated and sought-after speaker as well as a mother of three, Marsha agreed to spend her Mother's Day teaching the parents and students who gathered.

She did a bang-up job, and the whole morning went smoothly. But I cannot tell you the number of moms and dads who approached me afterward to express their thanks *and* their disappointment. Some had come to check out the new guy, wanting to see what kind of teaching their sons and daughters might be getting for the next couple of years. In all my planning, I had not even considered this possibility. And to tell the truth, I, too, felt a bit disappointed that I hadn't seized the opportunity to connect with so many parents and communicate my respect for the invaluable role of godly mothers.

I shared some laughs with warm-hearted parents who razzed me about not wanting to preach in the "lion's den." I was also reminded that many parents *are* interested in my vision for the ministry as well as my passion to present God's truth to students.

All this to say, if you want to know what is happening on a Sunday or during Bible studies or special events, talk to your youth pastor about coming by, or just drop in when you have a chance. If you miss the person you were hoping to connect with, try again! This is just part of the homework that may make you not only comfortable with what's happening at youth group but also *excited* about it.

Don't Ask, Don't Tell

Before we move on, I would like to share with you what can happen when parents not only don't do their homework but flat-out refuse to find out what's going on during youth-ministry hours.

When I worked with a youth ministry of about a hundred students in Colorado, our church sponsored an outreach event called The Lock-In. My staff and I challenged the students to invite every nonbeliever they knew. We also vowed that if they got five hundred people to attend, four of us leaders would shave our heads during the event.

For weeks students joked with me, telling me I had better be ready to lose my hair. I got more and more excited as the event drew near, anticipating that my students would actually meet the challenge our team had given them.

When the night arrived, the students brought more than five hundred kids to the all-night event and cheered wildly when, at midnight, my wife took a razor to my head. Shortly after this mania, a youth-pastor friend of mine presented the gospel, and more than eighty students made decisions for Christ.

As you can imagine, an event like this required *lots* of adult supervision. We needed parents to oversee a number of different stations, including the inflatable "toys" we'd rented—a bounce house, a jousting ring, a Velcro wall, and a laser-tag maze. We also knew that parents would be needed in the "video arcade," a room we'd stocked with PlayStations, GameCubes, and almost every imaginable portable electronic device. We provided snacks and basketball, board games and tournaments all night, so parents helped with these things. We had also set up a "cinema" downstairs, where many tired students crashed after playing for hours and hours, and we needed parent volunteers to keep an eye on the movie-going crowd.

At each of these stations, anywhere from one to three leaders provided security or helped supervise. My team and I had worked for weeks to staff the event with as many responsible adults as we could. The leaders also took turns making rounds, looking out for anything others might have missed.

While doing my sweep of the movie room at about three in the morning, I saw Desiree and her boyfriend snuggled together in the same sleeping bag. I don't know where the designated leader was when they crawled into that bag, but at that moment I wished I had appointed *ten* adults to guard the cinema station. Even worse, another leader told me that just two hours earlier he'd had to break the couple up after noticing Desiree and Chad giving each other sensual backrubs while waiting in line.

I woke the two up immediately and told them that they not only had to separate, but they also had to refrain from any physical contact for the last three hours of the lock-in. They both looked so shocked and offended I almost wanted to ask, "Are you kidding me?"

In my mind I reasoned, *They can't have assumed that I'd just turn the other way and let a couple of teens sleep next to each other in the church basement.* But when I broke things up, that's precisely what Desiree and Chad seemed to be thinking.

Chad didn't attend our church, but I looked for Desiree's parents Sunday morning when the lock-in ended. I couldn't find them, so when I arrived at the office on Monday, one of the first things I did was call their home.

Desiree's father answered, and I gave him the long and short of what had happened at the lock-in. He told me, "Well, her mother deals with this kind of stuff." From his perspective, this ended our conversation. Flabbergasted, I asked that his wife call me as soon as possible.

Not only did she never phone me, she and her husband made it known through the grapevine that they were outraged at my treatment of their daughter. Desiree, too, told people she just didn't like me.

I didn't try to defend myself. I felt justified in what I'd done, and I think many youth pastors and parents would have done the same. But this mom and dad seemed unwilling to hear anything negative about their daughter. They didn't ask her what she'd been doing and apparently didn't want me to tell them either.

It's not unusual for youth leaders to face this kind of response from parents. My boss shared that while working at one church, he'd had to confront a student's parents about the sexual misconduct of their son. Not only did the parents leave his office in an outraged huff, they left the church.

Most parents who pick up a book like this probably won't fall into the "don't ask, don't tell" category. But as a father, I also know I probably wouldn't *want* to hear about my daughter sleeping in the same sleeping bag as her boyfriend or about my son taking a relationship too far physically. However, I would encourage parents to both find out what's going on in youth group (like the mom and dad I mentioned earlier) and listen when someone tells them something—even a hard something—about what's going on during youth ministry. I pray that we all might be prepared to do our homework and find out whether our children are using youth group as an opportunity to sin.

A LITTLE GLIMPSE

I love going to wholesale stores like Costco, because they offer so many samples of what's available. You can almost get a full meal—appetizer, entrée, and dessert—if you shop at the right time. Over the pages that follow, I'd like to offer you some "Costco-size" samples of what a Sunday service, a midweek Bible study, a retreat, and a mission trip might look like in a typical youth ministry.

Before I start I have to make this disclaimer: These are only generic sketches of what might occur during a given youth activity. I don't know what youth ministries across the nation do from week to week, and even if I did, I couldn't present it all here. Yet having served at five churches and worked with, spoken at, or visited countless others, I've observed many patterns that are consistent with Bible-based youth ministries.

My hope is that these samplings will give you a little glimpse into the world of youth ministry. So here we go…

Youth Worship Service

A youth service typically lasts one or two hours, depending on the preaching, fellowship, and style of worship.

Many youth services start with prayer, either within the larger group or among the staff and those adult volunteers and students leading the morning's service. What follows is often a fellowship time during which students can mingle—and hopefully get all of their "heying" and hugging done before worship starts.

At some point a staff person or student leader opens the morning with a welcome. Visitors are introduced at this time and are encouraged to fill out a communication card. These cards ask for basic information, which enables youth workers to contact visitors the following week. Announcements follow, highlighting upcoming events, and then a call to worship is given, which may include a reading and application of Scripture.

Most youth groups transition at a certain point into a time of worship. Our church often begins with more upbeat music and winds down with meditative or contemplative choruses.

The preaching during student services will vary according to the season and need, as well as the personality of the youth group. Whether the teaching is expository or topical, a solid youth ministry will use part of the service to study the Bible.

Many youth groups (my own included) think it's valuable to instruct students in the discipline of giving, and an opportunity is provided during the service for young men and women to give back to God a portion of the money He has given them.

Mix It Up
Following are some of the ways youth groups "mix up" their worship services.

- Some groups use their worship services as an outreach and include an icebreaker game or an introduction to the group time.
- Others set aside time for students to meet someone new after the service gets started.
- Videos may highlight what's happening in the ministry and/or upcoming youth events. Sometimes a variety of media are used to introduce or highlight ideas in the morning message.
- Drama can be used for the same purposes.

- Special music (solo, choir, orchestra, or ensemble) may be used for similar purposes or during the offertory.
- Guest speakers may teach on a variety of subjects or Scripture passages. For instance, our church has a two-week missions conference every year, during which speakers present students with service opportunities or give updates on current service projects.
- Sometimes groups change up the format of their service to provide a break from the norm. For instance, if students are accustomed to worshiping first and then listening to teaching, flip-flopping the two might spark some new energy.

Small Group or Bible Study

Like many ministries, our youth ministry gathers on Wednesday nights for a midweek program. An event like this can last from one to two hours, again based on the student ministry's style.

Welcoming students and making announcements often come first. Then churches sometimes transition into a get-to-know-you or icebreaker game. My staff has definitely had fun creating wacky games for the students.

Like Sunday mornings, Wednesday night usually includes a time for worship. My staff likes to take anywhere from twenty to thirty minutes for this time, allowing students to reconnect with God after what might have been a tough day at school.

Our ministry also places a high value on small-group time, setting aside an hour for students to study the Bible, pray for one another, and encourage one another in their faith. This all happens under the loving leadership of a volunteer or staff person.

Some youth ministries reconvene the larger group after Bible-study time in order to wrap up the night. Some spend a shorter amount of time in small groups. What matters is not the *length* of time spent but the *quality*.

Mix It Up

Following are some of the ways youth groups mix up their midweek pro-grams. The "mix-ups" from the previous section definitely apply here as well.

- Switching locations often jump-starts a midweek program. Our youth group meets off-campus during the summer; some groups do this every week. (Leaders should make this information avail-able so you will know where your child's youth group gets together.)

- Some groups get together on alternative nights, apart from the main midweek program. At the churches where I worked, some students could not join the rest of the youth group on Wednes-day nights because of conflicting commitments. So their small groups decided to meet at a more convenient time or on a more convenient night.

- Different seasons may provide breaks from small-group or Bible-study formats. Often, summer events focus on connecting stu-dents with one another through social times with a short worship and teaching service. (We do barbecues, pool parties, and other fun events, for instance.)

- Sometimes groups devote an entire midweek event to worship and sharing. They may include Communion during such a time.

- Youth ministries sometimes sponsor classes in spiritual growth before the midweek program begins. For instance, I have taught a "fundamentals of the faith" class several times and love helping students grow in their knowledge of God.

- Some ministries hold prayer meetings before the midweek program begins. Usually the entire youth group is invited to participate in these times set aside to pray for students who have shared a special need or asked for prayer. Our prayer team often writes notes of encouragement to the people for whom they prayed that week.

Outline of an Hour

You may have noticed that during a midweek event, an hour or more can be devoted to small-group or Bible-study time. I'd like to give you a brief rundown of what this hour might include. I actually hand out an outline of an hour like this to all my leaders as they start discipling a core group.

- *Ten minutes—Make sure students know one another by name.* Have everyone share about his or her life in some way. Some leaders like to use a game or food to break the ice.

- *Forty minutes—Get to the Bible study.* Volunteers should prepare themselves for studying God's Word and be purposeful about it. It changes lives! Everyone in the group should interact, and a leader can encourage students, including the shy ones. The leader will try to use practical examples that apply to the lives of all the students. Some groups like to memorize Scripture, leave time for a Q&A session, or use teaching aids and object lessons.

- *Ten minutes—Prayer.* During this time students are encouraged to be vulnerable and give prayer requests. Leaders can pray that students will apply what they've learned during the study. In addition, if students do not know how to pray or are not comfortable doing so aloud, this might be a chance for them to learn.

Outreach Event

Since a major focus of outreach events is introducing nonbelievers to Jesus and then providing a place for them to grow in Him alongside other Christians, such gatherings might look a bit different from other church activities. An outreach event may last an hour, or it may go all night.

Remember the all-night lock-in event I described earlier? This event, which was heavy on fun, led up to a presentation of the gospel. In the first chapter I also talked about a coffeehouse outreach that focused on building relationships, yet climaxed with the sharing of a student testimony.

To give you a glimpse into an outreach activity, let me describe a weekly outreach I oversaw for about two years.

We'd begin the evening with recreation. Students who needed to get some of their pent-up energy out could do so readily, since we offered at different times (or sometimes simultaneously) softball, basketball, football, Nation ball, and even skateboarding. In fact, some of my students and leaders actually built skate ramps, which stayed in our church storage shed when not in use.

Some churches, like ours, have foosball and/or pool tables, air hockey, and the like. (These may seem to some parents like time-wasting diversions, but I have seen some *great* ministry happen around the foosball table.)

For those who liked less competitive, more relational activities, we had tons of board games as well as a café that offered food and drink for minimal prices. We sold candy, soda, and coffee shakes (like a very popular coffee store's blended drink that starts with a "Frap" and ends with a... Well, you can figure it out.) We did find, however, that we needed to limit the amount of snack foods we sold to certain students. I remember discovering that one junior higher had brought five dollars and spent all of it on Skittles, consuming the whole lot in just under an hour. (A note to all you healthy moms and dads out there: Someone did suggest bringing veggie trays as an alternative to candy, but that didn't really fly with students.)

After rec time, we brought students together and sang one or two songs that were easy to follow. After that we'd usually move into a skit, a multimedia presentation, or a class competition that highlighted the upcoming message. We once did a *Survivor*-themed contest, which the students loved. Brian Aaby, a youth-pastor friend of mine, spent hours developing one of his outreach retreats around another reality-TV series. Older students can also help take ownership of their youth group by acting in or leading these kinds of activities.

A shorter teaching time, maybe one that includes a gospel message, followed next, and then we would ask students to break up into smaller groups and talk about what they had just heard. Volunteer leaders helped facilitate these discussions.

The night ended much as it had begun, with recreation time before students departed for home—and maybe homework.

Mix It Up

Following are some of the ways youth groups mix up their outreach events:

- Some outreach events include only a short testimony rather than a time of teaching and a gospel presentation.
- Crazy activities, such as Jell-O battles, wet-dog-food fights, water wars, mud football, and so on, may be included. *Note:* These things are fun, but I see them primarily as memory-building activities. I want students to enjoy themselves, but games are never my main focus.

Creative Possibilities

During worship services, small group or Bible studies, and outreach events, pastors may utilize visual illustrations to support the teaching and mix things up.

For instance, after teaching on purity, I once used an idea of one of my creative interns, Anjuli. I invited the students to come forward, pick a rock out of a muddy pool, and then wash it in clean water at one of several basins around the room. This physical act signified that each student who washed a rock and placed it in a clean glass jar was making a commitment to the Lord and laying his or her purity before God. A lot of students liked and remembered this.

I once visited a worship service during which every member of the congregation was given a piece of jagged stone. The teaching that evening highlighted differences in the body of Christ and how every man and women is an essential part of the beautiful design God is creating through

His church. At the close of the service, people took their pieces of stone and glued them to a board, making a gorgeous mosaic.

During a recent worship and sharing time, my team suggested using muted television monitors to direct visual worship. They set up three screens, one that showed the miracle of God's creation in nature, one that displayed the depravity of man (we used film footage of the 9/11 disaster), and one that brought to life the death and resurrection of Christ (our choice was *Matthew*, produced by The Visual Bible).

My wife later told me that she and several others with whom she had spoken could not keep their eyes off the *Matthew* screen. The sights of Christ's suffering and triumph added to a powerful evening of personal worship.

Part of a Greater Body

I mentioned briefly that youth ministry is not a separate entity but rather an integral part of the body of Christ. As such, a youth ministry should reflect the goals and vision of the church with which it is connected. At EFCC where I now serve, our elders and pastors have spent much time delineating the specific purpose of our ministries. In one sentence, the overarching aim for our church is "to honor God through Christlikeness." Our youth group shares this goal.

A healthy youth ministry participates in fulfilling the vision of the greater church and accomplishing its purpose. I believe that students should be able to grow in their relationship with God, in their relationship with others in the family of God, in their relationships at home, and in their relationships with those outside the body of Christ. Young men and women should never feel disconnected from the larger congregation, which also shares these core values.

If you don't know whether your church has an articulated purpose, find out. Then determine whether those aims are carried out through the youth ministry. This relationship between youth ministry and the greater church is essential and should be part of what's happening.

ADVICE AND ENCOURAGEMENT

It's time for the rubber to meet the road. Here's some practical advice and encouragement that can help you find out what's happening at your church:

- Go to the parents' meetings, if they're offered. Many parents don't make time to attend meetings, but this is an important way to keep in touch with what's going on in the youth ministry.
- Check to see if the ministry has a Web site or a telephone hot line that provides information on current events and may articulate the vision of the youth group.
- Call the church secretary to ask about event calendars and other written information about the ministry.
- Make an appointment to talk with the youth pastor or director.
- Offer to chaperon an event.
- Just go! (Especially if you're concerned about a certain event or program.)
- It's great to ask your child what's happening at church, but *don't* just take his or her word for it! Students may misrepresent what's happening, particularly if they can see the youth group only through a certain grid. They may also be unable to verbalize what's going on.
- After doing some research, take a moment to establish if what you've determined about a ministry is accurate or if you simply want tighter control over your child or the church.

These tips may help a good number of you, but others may feel frustrated by them. *These would be great,* you may be thinking, *but I can't even tell who's in charge or where the youth group meets. It seems like things change with the tides, and I'm fed up!* If you feel this way, consider these suggestions:

- Don't assume the negative. Maybe things have been indeterminate for a good reason. (For instance, the group may not have a place to meet.) You could provide or find that place. Additionally, unforeseen things happen to all of us, youth pastors included. I once took a group of students ice skating, and when we arrived at the rink, we discovered that our registration had been lost. We had to "punt" and find something else to do. If a parent had shown up at the skating rink to pick up his son or daughter, he might have been frustrated and/or worried.

- Voice your concerns to any pastor at the church. If he can't answer your questions himself, he should be able to connect you with people who can.

- Remember that you don't have to just "go with it." Every youth ministry should have a level of responsibility and accountability. Parents should be able to know the who, what, when, where, and how long for events and activities.

- Drive your child (and a couple of his or her friends, if you have room) to each event. Ask a leader directly what the next activity is and where it will be held.

- If the youth pastor is not a gifted administrator and you are—or you know someone who is—volunteer to help out or encourage another person to do so.

- Again, after doing some research, take a moment to establish if what you've determined about a ministry is accurate or if you simply want tighter control over your child or the church.

Out of the Ordinary

Many churches offer retreats, camps, and mission trips in addition to the normal youth activities of any given month. These are great ways for students to connect with the ministry and to one another.

Hopefully there's a purpose for every event at your church. The goal may be as simple as fostering meaningful relationships and building memories, or it may be as deep as opening students' eyes to the need for world evangelism.

I support parents who allow and encourage their sons and daughters to participate in special events, because it's *vital* that they connect with other students. Just because there's less Bible study or worship happening at a given event does not mean your child won't benefit from it spiritually.

In fact, months after a water-skiing trip during which the spiritual emphasis was simply authentic fellowship, a girl approached me and thanked me because I helped her turn her life around. Curious, I asked her what specific thing had prompted her refreshed commitment.

"The water-ski trip," she answered.

I wanted to blurt out, "There was nothing special about that!" but I'm glad I didn't. This girl went on to explain that the relationships she'd started while water-skiing had made it easier for her to connect in a small group in which she grew in her understanding of God's Word and was accountable to others. Before the trip she felt disconnected, but afterward she felt like a vital part of the body of Christ.

A youth ministry should encourage fun as well as depth. I know that when I stand before God, He's not going to ask me how many water-skiing trips I planned and executed, but I'm sure He will be pleased that one girl's life was impacted by such an event.

During retreats, an emphasis on fun and relaxation may be combined with challenging messages. Small group or cabin discussions can also help students grow, commit their lives to the Lord, or recommit to following Christ. There may be structured quiet times during which students can study in greater depth what is being taught. There may be time for optional devotions as well. Sometimes worship through music will tie in with the teaching; other times it will focus on another aspect of knowing God.

Your church might also offer service retreats or short-term mission trips for students. For instance, in California, weekend trips to Mexico or inner cities are fabulous chances for students to serve and grow. Such retreats may help younger students transition to longer, more intense mission trips.

If your church provides opportunities for foreign or domestic youth missions, you'll need different information based on the nature of the travel. The following list of questions will help you do your homework on youth retreats and special events as well as on mission trips.

- Who is leading the trip? (Do they have experience? Are they spiritually and emotionally mature? Are they trustworthy?)
- What are the sleeping arrangements?
- What is the plan for transportation?
- How much will the event cost and will spending money be needed?
- How long will students be at different locations?
- Who are the other chaperons/leaders?
- What, if anything, will be taught/discussed?
- Do trip leaders have a specific plan for handling emergencies?

The following questions are specifically for mission trips:

- Which organization, if any, is the team partnering with? (This may depend on church connections and resources as well as relationships with individual missionaries. One set of parents did their homework and did not allow their son to participate in a foreign mission trip after viewing the organization's Web site. Another set of parents who wanted to send their daughter on a trip apart from the youth group asked my opinion on the group with which she wanted to serve, and after our talk, she signed up to go.)
- Are shots, visas, or passports required?
- Will your child need to raise financial support?
- How will the support money be used?

- What other information on the trip is available? (This includes flight times and dates, fund-raisers, ideas on raising support, pre-trip training and meetings, a list of special items needed, insurance [something like evacuation insurance may be required for overseas trips], emergency phone numbers, communication options, and a trip itinerary [including what the students will be doing, such as VBS, street evangelism, work with orphans, and so on]).

If your church does not offer mission opportunities, you may help your child find an organization with which he or she can serve. A wonderful family we know opted for this even though our church provided both domestic and foreign mission opportunities. This mom and dad wanted their daughter to serve with a group they had partnered with in the past, and I wholeheartedly endorsed their decision.

I hope this chapter has helped you better understand what typically happens at youth events. As you probably noticed, the responsibility for youth ministry lies with you as well as with youth leaders. It's the responsibility of youth leaders to provide you with necessary information about events and to be available to respond to your concerns. And it's your responsibility to find out what's happening so you can support the ministry and hold its leaders accountable.

What Parents Like You Had to Say

From Josie, mother of five, two married daughters and three children who currently participate in youth ministry:

My husband and I felt sad when our daughters told us they didn't want to attend youth group anymore. "It's so shallow," they claimed. Since we didn't know exactly how to respond, we decided to find out for ourselves what the student ministry at church really looked like. A short time later we began volunteering in the youth ministry. We absolutely fell in love with a particular group of junior-high girls. We wanted to follow them and, more important, our youngest son through high school. So when the time came for him to enter ninth grade, I started attending student services and always left feeling blessed. If I stopped going to youth group now, I could confidently say that what happens there is not shallow, but biblical and solid. I am very glad I took the time to find out for myself what's happening in our church's student ministry.

Three

Knowing the Leaders

WHEN I BEGAN writing this chapter, I wanted to relate two stories that demonstrate polar-opposite ways parents can get to know youth-group leaders. One situation is just plain ugly; the other is altogether good. I wanted to present both extremes, but I debated which situation I should describe first.

I ultimately chose to begin with the bad news, but in doing so, I don't mean to imply that the years your child participates in youth group will be fraught with difficulty for you or the youth staff. Instead, I want to balance the negative anecdote by following it with a powerful, positive example. Then we can jump into the rest of the chapter on a high note. With that said, let me tell you what happened in the dead of winter one year…

AMBUSHED

One Monday afternoon, about two and a half years into my ministry at one church, I received a call from a father I'd never met. His children wouldn't be old enough to enter the youth ministry for several years, but he expressed a desire to introduce his family to Jerusha and me.

The Randalls had only recently joined the congregation. Ed told me that he and his wife wanted to get to know the pastors and directors who worked with children (presumably because they had several kids). Jerusha and I tried to make ourselves as available to families as possible, so I told him we'd like to meet his family soon.

Graciously, Ed invited us to dinner at his home. For a few minutes he and I attempted to coordinate schedules. After a few unsuccessful attempts, I said that Jerusha and I could come on Thursday evening of that very week.

Ed seemed pleasantly surprised and asked if I was sure. At the beginning of our talk, I had mentioned that Thursday was my day off and that I tried to reserve that evening for time with my wife. Since I often had to be gone three or even four nights a week for ministry, Thursday evenings were precious to me. After my brief conversation with Ed, however, I thought dinner with this family would be an enjoyable and relaxing way for Jerusha and me to spend our night off.

A bitter cold front set in late Thursday afternoon, and Jerusha slipped while climbing the steps to the Randall home, so the evening didn't start out on the best note. Fortunately, Jerusha wasn't hurt and Ed opened the door, ushering us out of the biting cold and into a warm home.

Children poured down the stairs, running on top of one another in excitement to greet the guests. That's always a great way to start dinner with a new family, so I began to relax and settle in for a nice meal and an evening of fellowship.

When we turned the corner to enter the family room and kitchen area, Ed motioned to another couple and said, "I hope you don't mind. I asked the Dixons to join us tonight."

I have to be perfectly honest; this didn't thrill me. I'd only had a couple of interactions with the Dixons, and they hadn't seem pleased with the direction I was taking the youth ministry. They had four children, two of whom had already moved on to college and two who were in the youth group.

Wanting to give the Dixons the benefit of the doubt and make the best of whatever might happen, I extended my hand and introduced them to my wife.

We sat down to dinner almost immediately, the kids at a table apart from the six adults. A little chitchat bounced back and forth as we passed the spaghetti, salad, and garlic bread. Ed gave thanks, said amen, and without skipping a beat, shot this question at me: "So, Jeramy, tell me why you think it's a good idea to invite nonbelievers who engage in all kinds of immoral things to church where they might lead our kids astray?"

At first I hoped he was joking. I waited a second, thinking he might laugh and ask me a few get-to-know-you questions instead. I honestly thought his family wanted to meet Jerusha and me. Little did I know, however, that he'd planned a pig roast that night, and I was the pig!

After a brief, uncomfortable silence, during which I tried to collect my stunned thoughts, I began to explain my philosophy of ministry: A youth group needs both biblical discipleship and opportunities to share the good news with unsaved kids.

I didn't even get to share my heart for providing a safe place for unchurched students to connect with authentic believers. I never got to relate what I'd learned in studying the Gospels: Jesus didn't fear that interacting with "sinners" would pollute His disciples. Rather, He and His followers shared meals and conversation—much of daily life, really—with "unbelievers." Later, Christ told the apostles to take the good news to sinners everywhere, as far as the very ends of the earth. Our Lord never seemed to want the church to become a holy huddle insulated against "dangerous" outsiders.

Before I'd even gotten my first sentence out (the one about balancing discipleship and outreach), Ed interrupted, telling me that there were plenty of ways his kids could learn to evangelize, none of which included "building relationships."

I tried a couple more times to articulate my vision, but it became increasingly clear that he not only cared little for my hopes and plans for the ministry but also for me as a person. His heated intrusions on my every attempt to speak and his combative attitude made me feel not only defensive but disrespected.

Speaking for the Dixons, his wife, and himself (the other parents at the table spoke maybe one or two sentences each), Ed hammered me for about twenty minutes. Needless to say, I didn't feel like eating.

Ed deeply offended me. He invited Jerusha and me to his home under the auspices of getting to know us, but he pulled a bait-and-switch that caused us great pain. We gave up a special night of the week and got completely ambushed.

I know people will disagree with different aspects of my ministry vision as well as how I carry it out. I'm never opposed to parents coming to me with their concerns, questions, and even doubts about the youth group. I've served long enough to know that some conversations about the spiritual direction of young people will become heated, particularly when moms or dads think their church is missing the mark in ministering to students. But I don't like my wife having to listen to the tirades of incensed parents, and I want to protect her from bad feelings about these angry families. That's why I've set aside office hours for the purpose of meeting with happy *and* unhappy parents.

Finally, I broke in and put an end to the conversation. I told Ed that I felt offended that he'd asked me over to defend the youth ministry and my leadership of it. I also communicated that it was inappropriate for him to invite Jerusha and me to his home under the pretense of getting to know us, when all the time he was harboring different intentions. I expressed that the message he (and his wife and the Dixons) had communicated most clearly was that they didn't want to partner with me as a leader; they only wanted to change and control the ministry.

I rose from my chair and took Jerusha's hand to lead her out of the room. Ed stood as well, asking if he could pray for us before we left. Truth be told, I didn't want to hear his prayer. I didn't want to stay for another minute. But I knew that wouldn't be what Christ wanted, so I stayed (grudgingly).

The bad and ugly part of that evening wasn't that Ed Randall disagreed with me. It was that he didn't want to know me so that he could disagree with my goals respectfully. Instead, he just wanted to pin me to the wall.

After our get-to-know-you dinner with the Randalls, I couldn't separate Ed's comments from his lack of concern for my feelings and my commitment to ministry. If he'd taken the time to know me, or even if he'd used my office hours rather than my night off to express his views, perhaps we could have dialogued about his concerns. Instead, I felt alienated from him and found it virtually impossible to separate his ideas for improving the ministry from the contentious way he presented them.

True to the End

Leslie was one of the first mothers I met at Tri-Lakes Chapel in Colorado. In fact, as Jerusha and I prepared to fly home after our second candidating trip, Leslie and the rest of the Earle family spotted us in the Denver International Airport (DIA). On their way to Disney World, Leslie, her husband, and their two daughters stopped us at our gate to make sure we were taking the job. We told them we at least had to wait for church leaders to offer us the position—which they ultimately did.

Vivacious and hilarious, Leslie had an infectious energy that blessed me from day one. She quickly joined my curriculum-development team and agreed to teach a Bible-study series on the book of James.

Having battled cancer, Leslie knew lots about joyful perseverance through trials. Not only had she lived through fear and pain, she'd also endured the sometimes excruciating advice of "friends" who didn't approve of her choices, especially her decision to pursue a holistic healing path. Every one of my team members felt her journey would serve as a great example for the students.

And it *did*. Leslie taught with conviction, integrity, and transparency. I knew I liked this woman, even at the very beginning when I thought of her as the Disney World mom at DIA.

Leslie and her family invited us to their home a couple of months after we settled into our new home. Before I accepted her invitation to dinner, Leslie told me that she not only wanted to get to know me, but she also wanted to hear about what I hoped to do as a youth pastor. She explained that her family had been concerned about some of the things they'd seen in other ministries and that she'd like to give her input on the group dynamics at TLC.

I valued Leslie's opinion and had found her suggestions for the curriculum-development team insightful and pointed, yet always encouraging. I knew that even if she disagreed with some of my vision and philosophy, Leslie would articulate herself with dignity and class.

The time we spent with the Earles was a great mix of lighthearted fun and serious conversation. We laughed a ton, we all spilled dessert fondue on the tablecloth, and we shared stories of vacations, embarrassing moments, and so on. Yet we also hit on some tough issues—the exclusivity of the local high school and how that impacted the youth group, how students could easily slip through the cracks of a larger ministry, and how to plug students into leadership positions if they want to be involved but don't know where to serve.

Though we spent a good deal of time with the Earles that evening, our conversations about these topics didn't end. Rather, they expanded and deepened as Leslie partnered with me over the following months. She participated in trying some new things and worked alongside my entire team.

Because Leslie and I both had strong personalities and well-thought-out opinions, we didn't always see eye to eye. Yet we had the kind of relationship in which we allowed our disagreements to build us up. Furthermore, if other parents expressed a concern or suggestion, I could use Leslie, who knew me and understood my vision, as a sounding board.

During this time Jerusha and I also developed great relationships with Leslie's girls, both neat young women. We enjoyed ministering to them and cherished them dearly.

One afternoon our church secretary asked me if I could take a call from Leslie. I picked up the phone, but instead of hearing my friend's normally chipper voice, I heard a weak, tired version of it.

"Jeramy, I wonder if you'd be available to meet with me." She sounded as if she could barely choke back her tears.

"Sure. You name the time," I replied.

"Is right now okay?"

I cleared my schedule, and Leslie and I met shortly after her call. Through tears she told me she'd just returned from the doctor with her husband. Her cancer count had skyrocketed, and the prognosis looked grim.

At times like this I realize how heartbreakingly fortunate I am to minister not just to students but to their families as well. Leslie met with me because she and her husband viewed me not just as their daughters' pastor but also as their own.

I had the privilege of walking with Leslie through the hard months that followed. On a number of occasions, she asked me to talk with her girls about what was happening. Jerusha and I gladly hung out with Melissa and Emily now and then, especially when things got difficult at home.

Leslie's oldest daughter, Melissa, joined a team I led to the Ukraine and the Czech Republic the summer Leslie's cancer returned. When Jerusha and I got a message that we needed to phone Colorado as soon as possible, we found out that Leslie had been taken to a special treatment facility and neither she nor her husband would be there when our team came home. We knew this would crush Melissa.

Jerusha held Melissa's hand as I shared the news. Her tears broke our hearts, and my wife held her, loving Melissa as if she were our very own daughter.

Eventually Leslie went home to be with the Lord. I was in the hospice room with the family as she breathed her last. How agonizing those final moments were, yet how treasured they are now.

To the very end Leslie asked my family to share her family's life. She wanted to know us and be known by us. She invited us to love and help care for her daughters.

After Leslie passed away, our relationship with her family continued to deepen. We loved them—and still do. In getting to know us, Leslie and the whole Earle family made it easier for us to get to know and minister to them.

GETTING TO KNOW YOU

Of course I can't be as intimately involved with every family as I was with the Earles. And anytime a family disagrees with me or disregards my feelings, it won't always lead to such an ugly and inappropriate scene as my evening at the Randall home.

Yet these examples stand in sharp contrast to each other.

Leslie and her family made a conscious effort to know me and to participate in the youth group. The Earles made themselves available to serve and thus helped to shape the ministry through their involvement. They won a hearing with me through relationship and a clear commitment to providing the best for students at Tri-Lakes. Moreover, Leslie and her family shared their lives with me. I knew they cared about me personally, not just about getting in good with the pastor.

At the other extreme, the Randalls tried to manipulate and change the ministry through force. Without taking the time to get to know me or find out what was actually happening in the youth group, they attacked my ministry. They used a social time to make accusations and demands instead of using it as an opportunity to share their heart and vision with me.

It's a challenge to partner with families who don't seem interested in knowing why our ministry runs the way it does, asking about our ideas

and vision, or seeking to understand why our team has pursued a particular course, and trusting our sense of the Lord's leading.

Over the pages that follow, I'd like to encourage you to get to know
the leaders who work with your sons and daughters. Not only will you feel
more connected to the ministry and those who direct it, you'll also be able
to make informed decisions about when to support what's happening in
the youth group and when to challenge it. Knowing the leadership and
being known by them will give you a platform from which you can make
suggestions and offer help.

Furthermore, you'll have the opportunity to refresh the spiritual mentors God has given your child. Youth pastors and volunteers sometimes
run on empty, especially since they hear plenty of criticism and rarely
receive encouragement.

The Carnegie Council, a research organization on family-values
issues, recently reported to the nation that "a fundamental need of young
people...is for a stable, supportive bond with a caring adult."[1] Youth leaders are better able to provide that bond alongside parents who know them
and partner with them.

Finally, knowing the youth leadership can give you a clearer vision of
how your son or daughter might mature in the Lord during the tumultuous junior-high and high-school years. If you establish a relationship
with your children's youth leaders, you will be better able to keep track of
how your children are doing and what they are learning. You can then
reinforce at home the biblical principles they've been taught and the
Christlike attitudes they've seen modeled at church.

Allow me to offer you some practical advice on what to do and what
not to do when getting to know the leaders in your child's youth ministry
and letting them get to know you.

Definitely...

- Stop by the youth group and introduce yourself (and your
  spouse) to the leaders.

- Make an appointment to meet with the youth pastor during office hours.
- Call your son's or daughter's small-group or Bible-study leader and ask if you could introduce your family to him or her.
- Invite the pastor or leader to your home for an informal time of fellowship. (If your child is uncomfortable with this idea, you could meet at a time when he or she won't be home.)
- Invite the youth leaders to your child's sporting, school, and family events.

    (*A note on these first five suggestions:* Please respect the time that volunteer leaders sacrificially pour into your son or daughter. They might not be able to get together with you or with your child as often as you'd like. Keep in mind that they, too, have jobs, families, and other responsibilities.)
- Get involved with the youth ministry and watch the leaders in action.
- Be a friend to youth leaders. Send them Christmas, birthday, thank-you, or "just because" cards. (And a Starbucks gift card never hurts!)
- Show genuine interest in the youth staff and volunteers. Find out about their day-to-day lives, their families, their interests, and their goals.
- Find out if the youth pastor or leader has anything in writing about the ministry's goals and vision. You can learn a lot about someone through what he or she expresses in writing.
- If a purpose statement isn't available, you might exchange e-mails with the leader or set up a meeting after your initial introduction to ask the leader to share his heart for the ministry.
- Pray for the youth leaders! This is a fantastic way to feel connected with others. Ask them if they have any specific concerns for which you might pray, and then follow up with questions

about how God is answering your prayers. (Look for more on this in chapter 6.)

- Find out what kind of screening and hiring processes are used to select ministry leaders. This may reveal some things about your pastor or volunteer leaders. Finding out, for instance, where your youth pastor attended college and/or seminary may give you insight into his style and background. Knowing that volunteer leaders have to go through an application and interview process—perhaps even a background check—may give you greater confidence in who's supervising your son or daughter at church.

- Look for qualities you can appreciate about the leaders and point them out. An authentic relationship is built upon trust and mutual respect, so as you demonstrate your confidence in and esteem for the leaders, they may feel better connected to you and your child.

- If the leaders have proved themselves worthy of your trust, trust them. Assume the best about them and extend grace when they fail.

- Stay informed about how your child is doing at church. Periodic phone calls to the youth pastor and/or youth leaders can help you find out how things are going and if there's anything you can do to support them in shepherding your son or daughter. Leaders can better serve your child if they can partner with you and share their perspective on your son or daughter. A word to the wise: Pastors or youth leaders are often responsible for *many* students. No news doesn't always mean that things are going fabulously well. If asked by a parent, a leader may share some concerns that may not have been a big enough deal to call you about.

- Let the leaders know what your son or daughter is like at home. If there's a disparity between your child's behavior at home and at church, see if you can collaborate with youth leaders to help your child live more consistently.

- If you have criticism to offer, do it with gentleness and in a constructive manner (more on that in chapters 7 and 8). This approach will help you maintain as positive a connection with staff and volunteers as possible.

- If you have a problem with a volunteer leader, involve the youth pastor in the situation so that he can keep informed about the relationships between parents and his staff.

- Confide in the staff in an appropriate way. If you feel a leader should know specific things that might be embarrassing or painful for your child (for instance, a medical condition or past experience), exercise discernment and ask the staff person to keep such information confidential. Even if the leader is a personal friend of yours, let your son or daughter see that you can be trusted and will respect his or her desire for privacy.

If you would like to build or maintain a positive relationship with youth leaders, try *not* to…

- Expect too much of any one leader.

- Approach a leader with a concern over which he or she has no control. For instance, if you think a particular event was poorly executed, try to find out who planned it and go directly to that person rather than to his or her supervisor or the first leader you see. Going over someone's head can break trust and put him or her on the defensive.

- Talk to a leader about a concern in the middle of a ministry event when his or her primary focus is to serve students. Even if you don't run into a leader that often, make an appointment to speak with him or her at a more appropriate time. Also, it's best to wait until you have established some kind of rapport with a staff person before you offer criticism.

Letting Leaders into Your Family's Life

Many of the suggestions for getting to know a ministry's leaders also work for letting staff members get to know you. Typically, if you invite leaders to your home or to an event, not only will you get to know them, they will get to know you.

Do try to keep in mind, however, that you can't force your child to open his or her life to youth leaders. Also, remember that while you may be getting to know one or two leaders, the pastor or volunteers are very likely attempting to get to know *many* families. Try to maintain a gracious perspective as you invite leaders into your family's life.

When it comes to helping leaders get to know your child and your family, there are several things you can do and a few things to avoid.

Definitely...

- Allow your child to attend events (this helps leaders get to know your son or daughter).
- Participate in events yourself. If you chaperon, chauffeur, or volunteer, leaders will have a chance to get to know you.
- Hang around before or after youth events and, when possible, bring the rest of your family. Leaders will begin to recognize your family, which can eventually lead to a great relationship.
- Share about your life and experiences with leaders when appropriate. This will not only help them know you, but it will also give them better insight into how to relate to your son or daughter.
- Don't be afraid to be transparent with your son's or daughter's leaders. Intimacy begets intimacy, and as you share your heart, you make others feel safe to share theirs.
- Open your home for youth events. Leaders who come to your home are more likely to get to know you and your family.
- Take the time to dialogue with leaders who call you or want to give you information and/or updates.

On the other hand, try not to...

- Expect that a youth leader will pursue a relationship with you. Some volunteers and even some pastors are gun-shy since so many interactions between parents and youth leaders are negative.
- Assume that because of age, race, socioeconomic status, or anything else, a leader is ill-suited for ministry to your son or daughter.
- Overwhelm a youth leader. Respect a leader's time and thank him or her for serving.
- Expect a leader to be your new best friend or even your son's or daughter's best friend. As you well know, connections take time, and relationships are best built when time is spent together, ideas are exchanged, and experiences and memories are shared.
- Get to know leaders simply because you want them to do something for your son or daughter, such as treating your child specially or "saving" your child.

What Parents Like You Had to Say

From Jennifer, mother of two girls:

We wanted to get to know the youth leaders at church because the spiritual growth of our daughters was so important to us. We also wanted to be sure that our daughters were involved in spiritual-formation activities that were not just social in nature. And we really desired to be as supportive as we could. We appreciated so much the youth staff's consistency and commitment. We wanted them to know that if they had any questions or concerns, they could come to us. We tried to make our home available for special events and as a place of refuge for the youth workers.

Both girls made comments about their leaders' faithfulness over the years. In fact, the youth staff's devotion inspired my daughters to begin leading small groups of their own. Both of the girls' core-group leaders faced some hard times, but they didn't throw in the towel. Though high school is a hard stage of life, these young mentors stayed through the four years my girls were in high school. If leaders were to instill spiritual lessons in our daughters, we wanted to see that they had more than great words; we wanted them to live Christian lives before our daughters. So we got to know the leaders, and we found them to be authentic. We sought to know the leaders to the point that they felt confident we were interested in their personal lives. We didn't want them to feel as if we just buddied up with them so that they would treat our daughters well.

Jennifer's daughter Becca had this to add:

I liked having Krystal (Becca's core group leader) or Adam and
Katie (the high-school director and his wife) over for dessert
and board games. It was always fun, and I knew them better
than I would just seeing them at church. Our small group did
quite a few things outside of Bible studies, and by the time we
were seniors, we had a much deeper relationship than we did
at first or than we would have had if we'd only been together a
few times a month. Though I didn't know any of the youth
staff before I came into the ministry, by the end they weren't
just the "leaders," they were really my friends.

From Graham, father of two sons and a daughter, all of
whom participated in and graduated from the same youth
ministry:

I believe every father has a mandate from the Lord to act as
the primary discipler of his own children. Taking this role seriously and accepting it readily, I invested myself from day one
in the spiritual formation of my kids. Yet there came a time
when I knew that my children needed to hear the truth of
God's Word from others within the body. Whether it was
because my kids were testing their limits and asserting their
independence or because a "prophet has no honor in his
hometown," I recognized that the Spirit of God wanted to use
multiple voices to reinforce and communicate in fresh ways
what my wife and I had committed to teaching within our

home—the Lord's truth. Realizing this required that I release some degree of control and trust the body of Christ to partner with me in rearing my children.

As my sons and daughter entered junior high and high school, it became increasingly important that other godly mentors—not just my wife and me—speak into our children's lives. So I went out of my way to get to know those who were doing that spiritual "speaking into." The small-group leaders at church as well as the other paid and volunteer staffers were people I not only wanted to know but *needed* to know. My wife and I had personal contact with the youth workers and spent time outside of church with them, whether that time was at our home or at a school event. We attended the youth-ministry parents' meetings as a couple, and we always tried to talk directly with whoever oversaw the programs in which our children participated. I guess you could say we were highly proactive in getting to know the leadership.

Doing these relatively simple things afforded me the opportunity not only to pray for and partner with the leaders who helped form my sons and daughter spiritually but also appreciate what the leaders did week to week. Knowing them also allowed me to build a relationship from which I could express both gratitude and frustration when appropriate. [*Author's note:* See Graham's helpful comments on dealing with disappointment in chapter 7.] I would counsel all parents who desire to impact their children for Christ to know who speaks into their children's lives. The effort you make to know these people will most likely be richly rewarded.

From Vicki, mother of three:

I met Shelley for the first time at church, and my husband, Ron, served with her on a mission trip to Mexico. We both really liked her and were pleased when she became Jackie's core-group leader. The biggest thing for us was that Shelley stayed involved, discipling our daughter for all four of her years of high school.

I am now considering taking a core group myself, and Shelley has set an example for me. If I do choose to disciple a group, I want to make sure I can commit with the same long-term dedication Shelley had. Shelley continues to lead my daughter in a college Bible study, and I can't tell you what that has meant not only to Jackie but to our whole family. We love Shelley and hope to get to know her even better!

Four

Using Your Resources to Support a Youth Ministry

John had never worked with students, but when his kids entered junior high and wanted to be part of the youth group, he realized that God was calling him to serve his kids and their peers at church. He didn't necessarily feel that he'd fit best as a small-group leader; he thought he might be too old to connect with the students. But John quickly found ways he could support the youth ministry by using the resources God had given him.

You see, John and his family had brought a good deal of equity from California and had a fabulous home in the Colorado community where I worked. The outdoor trampoline, the megasized television hooked up with every video game you could imagine, and the full-size pool table made their home a perfect spot for ministry events.

Not only did John and his wife surrender their space on occasion after occasion, they also helped prepare food and kept their fridge downstairs stocked with soda. Students felt welcome and at home at the Baxters, which made it a great place for bonding events.

As you might have guessed from the description of the Baxters' home and toys, the family was blessed not only with the gift of gracious hospitality but with material resources as well. And John used his money to bless the youth group in some great ways.

The Greatest of Riches

Before we go any further, I want to establish one thing: You do not have to have loads of money—really *any* money—to support a youth ministry. I don't want any parents to think that you have nothing to give. All of us have resources we can share with a youth group.

The word *resource* can be defined as "an available means, a source of supply, expertise or information." *Webster's Dictionary* also includes these definitions: "a possibility of relief or recovery" and "an ability to meet and handle a situation."

Clearly resources don't exclusively refer to wealth or possessions. Your time, your energy, your abilities, and your experiences are all resources. Your passion for certain things and your personality are also means and sources of supply.

I particularly like the definition "a possibility of relief or recovery" because, as a youth pastor, I often need help. When a parent jumps in to serve, I am relieved that I can recover some time and energy for ministry.

Some of the best ways a ministry can be supported require little, if any, money. In the remainder of the chapter, I will outline ways others like you have served. Some parents have used their money, but many have given of their time, energy, and love.

For example, I had the privilege of getting to know the Langdon family. Missionaries who had recently returned from Southeast Asia, the Langdons didn't have much money. They also didn't feel a calling to volunteer with students. With three teenagers at home, they had their hands full already.

But like John's family, the Langdons found they could serve the youth group in other ways. Linda fixed numerous meals, blessing the students with her culinary skills and her delight in sharing them. Vince and Linda also opened their home for mission-trip meetings. Linda told me later what a privilege it was for her to help students go on outreach trips. The Langdons supported the youth ministry with both their passion and their gifts.

My friend Anthony, a former youth pastor in Arizona, once told me the story of a family who came to his office and asked, "What could the youth group really use?" (By the way, apart from asking "How can I know Jesus personally?" this is probably the best question someone can ask a youth minister.)

After catching his breath, Anthony replied that he'd love to outfit the youth room with some foosball and air-hockey tables. A lot of ministry happens during playtime, he explained. Right then and there this mother and father wrote a check for some recreation tables.

At different churches in which I've served, a number of families donated couches for our coffeehouse. These were not necessarily wealthy families buying brand-new sofas for their homes and dropping their old ones off at the church. People who couldn't give monetarily shared the things they either couldn't use anymore or simply felt led to give.

A mother of two didn't know how she could use her family's resources to support the youth ministry. She didn't have room in her budget to donate money directly to the youth group, but she had great organizational skills. So she headed up a group of women who set up an "agape dinner" for the students before the Sunday-evening youth service. Not only did the food break the ice for newcomers, it also gave the whole evening a real "family" feel. The other mothers under her leadership brought the food, set it up, and then cleaned up afterward. What a gift they gave week after week.

Another mom once met with me to tell me that she and her husband felt that God wanted them to donate their fifteen-passenger van to the church. A couple of their kids would be leaving for college soon, and they knew that the youth group could use the car more than they could. After explaining what she felt God prompting her family to do, this mom watched me open my prayer journal to the pages where I'd asked again and again (over eight months) for God to give us a van. He is faithful, and others get to help make His provision possible. How amazing is that? Up to that point, our ministry had been relying on parents to either drive students to events or loan us their cars. When we got the van, we could always count on room for fifteen in one car. In one fell swoop, this family's gift eliminated the need for three parent-driven vehicles.

Families from all tax brackets have helped me with registration for events or check-in on the day of youth activities. Without their help at those times, our staff would be pulled in far too many directions.

One summer, the Davises, who had a son in the youth group, lent us their boat for a couple of water-ski trips. Mickey drove the boat around for hours, teaching kids to ski, wakeboard, and kneeboard. He also pulled his share of inner-tubers, many of whom gleefully skidded across the water when he swirled them around the lake.

Though we never took them up on their offer when we lived in Colorado, Greg and Sheri told us we could use their camper for any retreat or activity. As a father now, I can see the benefit of housing my wife and toddlers in a camper rather than a tent. If only this family had moved with me to California!

Another mom who worked well with numbers kept track of the money for a mission trip I led to the Czech Republic and the Ukraine. Each of my students wrote support letters, and dealing with all the funds that came in over the two months before our trip would have definitely taken me away from other ministry opportunities.

The Jordans, who owned a cabin in the mountains, allowed our youth group to stay free of charge during a prayer-and-fasting retreat. How grateful we were for the quiet solitude of their Rocky Mountain home. It proved to be an ideal place for us to praise and seek God.

One of our devoted moms made personalized luggage tags for each of the students on one of our mission teams. Peggy laminated them at the church (combining her skill and time with what was available to her) and even made sure the tags would be visible from a distance. They were fluorescent yellow!

After one parents' meeting, during which I'd expressed the desire to upgrade the youth ministry's multimedia and computer equipment, a check showed up in my box for the amount I'd mentioned these items would cost.

Business owners have often donated their resources to support youth ministries I've led. For example, a father who co-owned a T-shirt business gave us—at cost—sixteen polo shirts embroidered with the mission-team logo a student designed. These shirts probably would have cost us forty bucks apiece at a retail store.

Two contractors helped me and a band of eager-to-destroy-things teenage guys demolish and then remodel the basement of our church to make a home for our youth group. We had been meeting in the sanctuary up to that point, but after we rebuilt things, the students had a place of their own.

During that same remodel, Randy, who owned a tile shop, donated his time and skill, his equipment, and even his connections to help us install granite countertops as well as tile flooring for our café area.

A dad who once did video editing for a living helps me now and then to create multimedia presentations and video skits. The students love the out-of-the-norm things he can do.

Another friend of mine, Todd, works really well with sound and camera equipment. He takes pictures at many of our events and comes faithfully (with a box of doughnuts) to lead the student tech crew.

A father who knows about television helped me set up a live feed during one summer youth event so the students could see themselves during the welcome time. As I'm sure you can imagine, they loved being on camera.

An architect whose kids aren't even in the youth group anymore wanted to help me draw up plans to update our current youth building. I couldn't have been happier when he offered to use his resources and abilities to help in this way.

Several parents volunteered to serve on the search committees that brought me to both Tri-Lakes Chapel and Emmanuel Faith Community Church. For the gift of their time and energy I will be eternally grateful.

So many parents have offered to drive for youth events, I couldn't recount the stories. One father even drives a bus to camp every year (a three-hour round trip for him). Let me add, if any of you have a bus license and attend a church large enough to have a bus, I highly encourage you to call the youth pastor and let him know you'd be willing to drive. Since a relatively small number of people have a bus license, my staff and I are always relying on the same folks. (By the way, anyone can get a bus license, so if you have a hankering for one, go get it!)

Lots of moms and dads have also served as counselors at camps and retreats. In fact, a woman who had a powerful encounter with God at a camp in California fifteen years ago returned to the same camp with her husband to minister to students.

Week after week, Liz McDaniel, a mother of two, mans the youth resource table (the home for flyers, Bibles, and other things for students who need them). Liz continually blesses our ministry. With a warm smile and sometimes a motherly hug, she greets students as they enter the youth room.

A dad who just loves to praise, Mike deNeve volunteered to head up a student band, teaching them how to lead worship. He develops their skills as musicians and ministers.

Janice Price, a mom who is passionate about praying for others, regularly meets with students to pray before Wednesday-night Bible study. She also helps the prayer team write personal notes of encouragement to each person who submits a prayer request.

What I've spent the last few pages trying to illustrate is this: There are an infinite number of ways you can use your resources to support a youth ministry. Chances are, if you can do something—*anything*—a student ministry can benefit. If you can cook a mean lasagna, your culinary skills can be used! If you can paint a wall or clean a counter, a youth ministry can use you. If you can plan or organize events, a ministry can definitely use you. If you have things lying around the house, a ministry can use them. Well, most of them. A family once approached me and offered to donate a weight set to the youth group. I declined, not wanting to turn the student room into a twenty-four-hour fitness club.

The point is, God has equipped us all in different ways. We can bless one another and those we serve by using our gifts. Parents usually want to see the youth program at their church thrive. *You* can support a student ministry by using your resources! All of us have unique information to give, expertise to loan, and abilities for handling different situations. We merely need to learn how to use our gifts. In his book *The Purpose-Driven Life,* Pastor Rick Warren discusses how we can do this by using our God-given "SHAPE" (spiritual gifts, heart, abilities, personality, and experience).

In the following sections, I share how parents can apply these five broad categories to support a youth ministry.[1]

Spiritual Gifts

The phrase *spiritual gifts* often confuses Christians. Although everyone who trusts in Christ is given spiritual gifts, some people fear they don't have a gift because they don't "feel" like an evangelist, teacher, prayer warrior, or missionary. This is simply not true!

Someone who can clean countertops with a cheerful spirit may have the gift of service. A person who can visit hospitals and cry with hurting people probably has the gift of mercy. People who can trust God despite difficult circumstances likely have the gift of faith. Those who cannot resist donating money to orphans and widows or causes for which they are passionate may have the gift of giving.

If people say, "You're so organized and efficient," you may have the gift of administration. If someone tells you, "You always seem to know what to say and consistently have a Bible verse to share," God may have gifted you with wisdom, knowledge, or encouragement. If you're known for your servant's heart, you probably have the gift of helps. Some people learn that they are gifted in a particular area because others point things out to them.

I encourage you to talk to your pastor about taking a spiritual-gifts test. While these tests do not identify your abilities, they are helpful tools to help you discern what gifts God has given you.

Finally, don't get too caught up in determining your spiritual gift before you start to serve. Most often, when people jump in to help the church, a God-given spiritual gift becomes evident.

Heart

Everyone feels passionate about something. Whether it's sports or babies or something else, most people get fired up about some things and not others. We all have a heart for something.

You may feel a strong love for students and want to get involved in their lives. (If so, make sure you check out the next chapter.) You may love to open your home for youth-group parties and get-togethers.

The things you did well and *enjoyed* doing in the past probably express your heart. Whether you've used these gifts recently or some time ago, you can minister with your "heart" abilities in a variety of ways. For instance, maybe you loved to put on shows when you were a kid. You made your own costumes and transformed your playhouse into a theater. Well, you might consider leading a group of students in presenting a live Christmas or Easter reenactment. You may even want to go as far as developing a drama team.

Perhaps you had a short-term job that equipped you with a particular skill. I worked for a short time as a contractor's assistant and developed skills that have helped me not only at home but also in ministry.

Because God loves us, He often gives us passion for and delight in the things He wants us to accomplish.

If you feel passionate about getting young people involved in drug-prevention ministries, you may want to ask the youth pastor if you can recruit some students to be part of such a program. Perhaps you feel passionate about supporting prolife ministries or helping the poverty stricken. You could encourage students to join walks for life or sponsor a child in a Third World country. One year the senior class in our group helped support an orphan, and they changed one little boy's life.

Look not only at what you like doing with your time and abilities but also at what makes your heart beat faster when you think about it. Both of these things reveal your heart, and both can be used to support a youth ministry.

Abilities

You probably have developed certain abilities from your work experiences inside or outside the home. Some abilities are artistic, some technical, and others vocational. Some abilities grow out of hobbies or recreation activities, while others spring from business experience.

Again, *anything* may be used to support a student ministry. Recently a student and her parents organized a golf outing. Skills in Web-site development, landscaping, professional or lay counseling, and carpentry are also useful for a youth ministry.

Several years ago parents at Emmanuel Faith began teaching sign language to young people. They now have a thriving ministry that often presents special "signing to music" performances and provides interpretation for the hearing impaired during youth services.

Every year a group of parents goes up to Hume Lake, a Christian camp ministry that serves thousands of students each summer. These men and women do the grunt work of cleaning, repairing, building, and gardening.

Parents who work in medicine volunteer to serve as nurses during youth retreats or camps.

Each of us is able to do *something* to support youth ministry. As we use our skills to impact the students in God's kingdom, many will be blessed.

Personality

There is no right or wrong temperament for ministry. Introverts and extroverts, thinkers and feelers can all benefit a youth ministry. Those who feel most comfortable with routine and those who like variety can serve effectively. People who enjoy challenging the status quo as well as those who prefer to work cooperatively "within the system" can use their personalities to support a youth ministry.

Many personality tests are available should you want to nail down your personality type. Although these tests can be useful, they are sometimes unnecessary. Most people know their basic personality type after the categories are explained.

Extroverts gain energy from interacting with people and seem to work best in a group, which enhances their creativity, enjoyment, and productivity. Introverts prefer interacting with only a few people at a time, gaining energy from introspection, quiet time, and solitude.

Thinkers tend to be analytical and fact-oriented when making decisions, while feelers most often make decisions based on how they sense the group may be affected by a choice.

Routine-oriented people usually like to be involved in activities in which they have a clearly defined role, are able to complete tasks, and can experience closure. And those who enjoy surprise parties, have several things going on at once, and like their roles to change periodically land in the variety-oriented camp.

Cooperative people work well with others and love to be part of a team in which they can hear various points of view. They work well with others to improve the way a ministry functions. Challenge-oriented people like to overcome obstacles by finding fresh solutions and trying new methods. Change often enhances their efforts and effectiveness.

All of these personality types are needed to make a youth ministry run smoothly. Get to know yourself and consider how you may be able to use your personality type to bless students.

An extrovert may be a great event leader or small-group discipler. An introvert could be a great prayer warrior. A thinker may be able to work through things that stump others, and a feeler will add the sensitivity to a ministry that young people need.

Routine-oriented people form the backbone of a youth ministry through their faithful service. Variety-oriented folks are willing to try new things and jump into aspects of ministry that need fresh blood or leadership.

Finally, cooperative people help maintain and deepen established programs and purposes. They consistently promote unity and consensus. Challengers move a youth ministry forward by helping the group overcome adversity with energy and vision. They promote change (even change that's initially unpopular) that will help strengthen a group's aims and activities.

Experiences

A former youth minister and respected author once told the story of a man who approached him sheepishly and said that God had called him to youth ministry. The man was bashful because he felt he had nothing to give. "I dropped out of high school and ran away from home when I was sixteen," he confessed. "I have no idea how *I* can help teens."

This man's experiences, painful though they were, helped support a ministry in some powerful ways. He could connect with troubled and at-risk kids who might otherwise have felt unable to relate to youth leaders.

Perhaps you've overcome struggles with substance abuse. Think of the number of students you could help who face the day-to-day temptations of smoking, drugs, and alcohol.

Maybe you've been a victim of abuse and understand the hurts some young people feel as a result of physical, emotional, or sexual traumas. Perhaps you struggled with an eating disorder when you were in junior high or high school. Your service could be invaluable to young people.

Not all experiences need be painful to be profitable. Your vocational experiences, your educational experiences, your spiritual experiences, and your past ministry experiences can all be used to support a youth ministry.

Maybe you've been trained to provide for the special needs of those who are physically challenged. Perhaps you've had instruction in accounting or a foreign language. These skills and experiences can certainly benefit a youth group.

Meaningful times you've had with the Lord and lessons you've learned through Bible study and prayer may also help students. If you've been baptized or learned how to tithe, you can help students see the value in doing these things.

Finally, you may have served in a church ministry in the past. Perhaps you headed up a small group of adults. Maybe you hosted some events, served in the library, or worked as a financial advisor.

Any ministry experience can be transformed or used by God to bless a group of students. Again, consider what you've done in the past and pray about how you might use these experiences to support a youth ministry. The Lord will use your experiences for His glory.

A Sample Handout

In closing I would like to give you a very practical tool that you or your youth pastor may be able to use.

At every parents' meeting, I hand out a Parent Involvement Sheet that lists some ways parents can serve a youth ministry without volunteering as a small-group leader. I encourage parents to look at the options, pray about them, analyze their spiritual gifts, and *call us!*

I first ask for a parent's name, phone number, mailing address, and e-mail. I also ask parents to list any children who may be involved in the youth ministry. This information enables me or my staff to easily contact a family, and it gives me the opportunity to put a student's face with his or her parents' names.

Then I list some potential ways moms and dads can become involved in the youth ministry. Each item has a box next to it so that parents can check off areas of interest before returning the sheet to me.

Some of the areas of service include:

- event planning
- meal preparation, catering, and so on
- administrative work
- construction
- cleaning
- hospitality (I further break down this area of service by asking, "How many students would you be willing to invite to your home?" I then list four to twenty-five-plus options.)
- donation or loan of the following:
  - digital camera or camcorder equipment
  - computer equipment
  - video game stuff
  - foosball table
  - air-hockey table
  - Ping-Pong table
  - sports equipment
  - espresso machine
  - blender
  - board games

- cabin
- motor home
- van
- ski boat
- pool/spa
- driving students to an event
- obtaining a special-vehicle license to drive students to events
- chaperoning a one-day event
- chaperoning a retreat
- leading a ministry team—drama, worship, multimedia, missions, events, prayer, etc.
- donating money directly to the youth ministry
- other (the catchall category, since I can't name *everything!*)

I give this sheet to parents to get them thinking and to help them see the great needs we have in youth ministry. True, some of these are not *essentials* (though, as I have mentioned, things like foosball tables can make for great ministry opportunities), but many are dire needs.

At the bottom of this sheet, I provide parents with pertinent information about the youth ministry: the church address as well as names, telephone and fax numbers, e-mail addresses, and office hours of paid staff members. This gives parents most of the information they need to get in touch with the ministry. Because I have more than forty volunteer staff people, I do not give their personal information to every parent. I do, however, encourage my leaders to share their telephone numbers and e-mail addresses with the families of the students they serve.

If your youth pastor doesn't have anything like this Parent Involvement Sheet, perhaps you could meet with him and discuss the possibility of developing a sheet that's tailored to your area. (For instance, there aren't many backyard pools in Colorado.) If he doesn't feel willing or able to do this, you could ask his permission to head up the collection and distribution of such information. I'm sure it would encourage him if, as a result of your work, people volunteered to support the ministry with their resources.

I'll summarize this chapter by saying that you *can* help the youth ministry with your time, your energy, or your money. Your passions, your personality, your experience, and certainly your spiritual gifts can also support a youth ministry if you are willing and able to serve.

I pray that God will reveal to you the ways He's gifted you for ministry. I also pray He will help you use any and all of your resources to support the youth group at your church.

What Parents Like You Have to Say

From Sue, mother of two sons:

Years and years ago my husband and I taught Sunday school, but as our boys got older we backed off from that kind of role. We remained very involved in their school activities but wanted to give them some space at church. Even though we didn't formally disciple students in the youth group, we did open our home and used what God had given us (including our hot tub and ski boat) to encourage the youth ministries. Our attitude was always "Let others enjoy what God's blessed us with." Sure, we've taken some "risks" in allowing others to share our things. A student once cracked a piece of our spa, for instance. I guess we could have been upset about it, but my husband and I feel that no matter what happens to our things, it's always worth taking a chance in order to minister. And let me tell you, the payoffs have been great. Not only did I get to know my sons' friends and, in time, their friends' families, but I also found that I connect well with young adults. After the boys graduated from the youth ministry, I jumped on board as a sponsor and then as a small-group leader.

Five

Partnering with a Youth Ministry

SCRIPTURE CLEARLY REVEALS that, with God's help, parents shoulder the primary responsibility for directing their children's spiritual growth and development (see Deuteronomy 4:9; 11:19; Proverbs 22:6; and Ephesians 6:4). As I write this, I'm struck by the awesome weight of the task and the incredible privilege it is to teach my own daughters to know and enjoy the Lord.

No matter how wonderful a Sunday-school teacher may be, this man or woman cannot impact your children for Christ like you can. No matter how powerful his sermons, the senior pastor will not teach your children the ways of the Lord like you can. And no matter how dynamic and godly the youth leaders are, they cannot bear the full weight of guiding your son or daughter along the path of righteousness.

YOUR ROLE AS "YOUTH LEADER"

While doing the research for his book *Soul Searching: The Religious and Spiritual Lives of American Teenagers,* sociologist Christian Smith interviewed thousands of thirteen- through seventeen-year-olds between 2001 and 2004. In a 2005 interview with *Books and Culture,* Smith disclosed two of his findings, which I believe are particularly pertinent to this chapter.

First, Smith discovered that most teens answered the question "What thing would you like to change about your family, if anything?" with these words (which may shock many of you): "I wish I was closer to my parents."

Wow! Let that sink in for a moment.

When asked why they aren't closer to their parents, teenagers replied, "I don't know how."

Young people may not "admit [to their parents] that they look to [them] for guidance, but...they do. Parents have a lot more influence, and therefore, responsibility than they realize."[1]

Smith also reveals that a vast majority of teens are "incredibly inarticulate about their faith, their religious beliefs and practices."[2] And even if young Americans can say something about their faith, they seem unable to connect their beliefs to the rest of their lives.

Reading *Soul Searching* could leave parents depressed, but it could also make us incredibly excited. For as we put these findings together, we realize that our children *want* to be close to us and, in fact, *need* us to be close to them, so that we might teach them about genuine faith and how it impacts daily life.

Throughout the Bible God charges parents with this task: "Train a child in the way he should go, and when he is old he will not turn from it" (Proverbs 22:6). Phrased another way, parents can teach their children "to choose the right path, and when they are older, they will remain upon it" (NLT).

As Christian parents we desire that our children would remain on the right path all of their days. We pray fervently that they would not turn from the Lord's ways. This verse in Proverbs suggests that early training can influence a child's lifelong character and choices.

Sometimes the job of "spiritual parenting" feels overwhelming if not impossible. Yet we begin training our children by humbly admitting we cannot do it by ourselves, remembering what the Lord has revealed to us, and trusting in what Scripture promises.

God instructed Israelite mothers and fathers, "Don't forget anything of what you've seen. Don't let your heart wander off.… Teach what you've seen and heard to your children and grandchildren" (Deuteronomy 4:9, MSG).

As you recall what God has done for you and as you stay firmly rooted in Him, your children (and *their* children) will see the Lord's power and grace. Sons and daughters must choose for themselves whom they will serve, but through coaching and directing, parents can help their children make godly choices.

It excites me when I consider that, as a youth minister, I get to come alongside families who want to raise godly kids. I have the privilege of sometimes encouraging, sometimes equipping, sometimes providing resources for parents. While I cannot be a child's primary spiritual mentor, I can work with parents and other godly family members.

Parents can use their child's youth-ministry experience to further his or her spiritual development. Moms and dads can also maximize the potential influence of youth group on their child not only by knowing what's being taught but also by discussing it with him or her.

Before you write this off with thoughts like *When in the world am I supposed to fit that into our family's frantic schedule? How could I even start a conversation about that?* or *My student won't even talk to me about the weather; how are we supposed to discuss spiritual things?* let me give you an example of how this can work. Then we'll look at some practical ways you can jump into training your child by partnering with the youth ministry.

MORNINGS WITH RICK AND BRANDON

For some reason, one Monday morning Rick asked his son Brandon, "So, what did you learn at church yesterday?" It seemed like a question a parent might ask a four- or five-year-old after Sunday school. Rick didn't anticipate this would spark a deep discussion about spiritual things.

But *God* knew. He knew that Brandon yearned to know more. God knew that Brandon hungered for the truth and the grace of His Word but couldn't articulate his need.

From that day forward, Rick and Brandon would talk about what Brandon had learned at church during their car rides to and from school. Brandon would read from the passage he had studied in small-group Bible study and then ask questions to deepen his understanding. Rick would also direct Brandon to other passages that would shore up the truths his son learned.

Both Rick and Brandon loved this time together, and both grew through it. By the time Brandon transitioned into the high-school ministry, I saw major changes in his knowledge of Scripture and his heart for God. When Brandon left the youth group four years later, he chose to be involved in ministry on his college campus.

Brandon's story isn't finished yet. Along with Rick, I pray that Brandon will stay on the right path and not turn from the way he should go. But no matter what choices Brandon makes, I know that Rick honored God in "making the most of every opportunity" (Ephesians 5:16) to teach and direct his son.

It Takes Some Work

I'm sure that every parent will have a different reaction to that anecdote. Some of you may feel like talking with your child *today.* Starting right now, you want to seize every chance you have to discuss spiritual matters with your son or daughter.

Others of you may feel as if a load of bricks has been dropped on you. You feel guilty that you haven't tried harder to parent your child spiritually, and you're fearful that there's no way you could do what Rick and Brandon did. You wonder if you'd be able to get three words out of your distant, moody student.

If you're scared to death, I want to remind you that "everything is possible for him who believes" (Mark 9:23). I also want to share with you an amazing prayer, offered by the prophet Jeremiah when he faced a seemingly insurmountable task: "Ah, Sovereign LORD, you have made the heavens and the earth by your great power and outstretched arm. *Nothing* is too hard for you" (Jeremiah 32:17, emphasis added).

Make this your daily petition, minute by minute. The Lord *longs* to help you teach your child the way he or she should go. He *yearns* to come to your aid as you train your son or daughter to walk with Him.

To both the "ready for action" and "totally unsure" moms and dads, I offer the following rubber-meets-the-road tips to help you maximize the potential impact of what's being taught at youth group. I pray that these suggestions will open a whole new way to equip your son or daughter for righteousness.

Keep in mind that all of these suggestions require some effort on your part. Spiritual parenting takes time, skill, and determination. As most of you know, raising kids is *not* for the faint of heart. But I believe that as you ask the Lord to give you the perseverance and energy you need and as you faithfully seek to apply the things you've learned, not only will you see fruit, but the task will get easier.

1. *Start with your own relationship with God.* You will not have anything to give your child if you don't cultivate your own intimacy with God. As you draw near to the Lord, as you read His Word, and as you pray, you will be better equipped to instruct and guide your son or daughter. If you notice that the time you spend with your child has become dry, do a quick check to see if you've strayed from God's ways.

2. *Gather the information you need.* In order to talk with your child about what's being taught at youth group, you need to *know* what's being taught. The simplest way is to ask your child, but if he or she doesn't remember or doesn't care to share with you, you can attend parents' meetings, check on

the Internet or youth-event calendar to find out about upcoming classes, or call the church office and speak with a staff member who can give you an idea of the teaching schedule. Knowing what's being taught will allow you to prepare your own thoughts for any time you might have with your son or daughter. (As an added bonus, getting this information will also help you make sure that something biblical and significant is being taught during the youth service and/or small-group Bible study.)

3. *Be creative.* If your son or daughter is more interested in talking about what's going on in life than what's being taught at church, ask the youth pastor to recommend a book or Bible study that might dovetail with his teaching or with what your child is interested in discussing. Many Christian growth books provide study questions at the back of the book. These can be great springboards for conversation.

4. *Be sensitive.* There will be times it just won't work to talk with your son or daughter about the Lord. Your relationship with your child will ebb and flow, and you can relax in knowing that it's the direction you're walking that matters to the Lord. Some days your son or daughter may want or need to talk to you about something entirely unrelated to the topic you've been discussing. Try to be sensitive to your child's needs and desires.

5. *Prod gently.* You cannot force your child to respond to you. Turning your conversation into a "You will answer me or you'll be grounded" ultimatum may push your son or daughter away from you and the Lord. Instead of trying to control his or her participation, look for open doors to interject thoughts about how a relationship with God might influence a particular situation.

6. *Be persistent.* Things may not go smoothly at first. You may get weird looks or heavy sighs from your child that scream, "What in the world are you thinking?" Keep trying! If you get absolutely no response from your son or daughter, use the time to share what *you're* learning (without preaching at him or her) or what you think about the topic being studied in youth group. It may take some time for your child to open up. He or she may *never* open up during the junior-high and high-school years. But your faithfulness to make the most of every opportunity will please the Lord.

7. *Find time in your schedule.* Yes, it takes time to talk to your son or daughter about spiritual things, but don't despair if you feel the pressure of an already overburdened schedule. Look for "teachable moments" like the following, which may easily fit into your daily life.

   • Like Rick and Brandon, you may have a long car ride to school, which is a great time to connect with your child. But even a five-minute ride in the car, when lovingly focused, can be a great time for connecting. (And it will send your child off to school on an encouraging note.)

   • If you already set aside time for family devotions, you could give your son or daughter an opportunity to share with the family what he or she is studying at youth group. As your child shares these things with others, the truth will sink deeper into his or her mind and heart.

   • You can also talk with your child during car rides to and from church, particularly right after church when spiritual lessons may be fresh in his or her mind.

   • At the lunch table after church or the breakfast table the following day, you can ask your son or daughter questions and help apply youth-group lessons to daily life.

- You can do all of these things as often as you'd like or alternate between them so your child doesn't feel forced into a rigid schedule.

8. *Lean on others.* There may be seasons during which another member of your family (an older sibling, an aunt, a grandfather, etc.) or a cherished friend can offer your son or daughter spiritual guidance that might not be accepted from you or your spouse. Perhaps these trusted ones can help you gain some perspective on and insight into your child. Maybe they can simply offer you a listening ear or a shoulder on which to cry. Whatever the case, lean on these invaluable friends and family members whenever possible. As our editor Shannon articulated it, "In this day of alternative family roles, extended family can be as responsible as immediate family" for encouraging a young person's spiritual growth. Encourage your son or daughter to develop meaningful relationships with extended family members who may have an influence for Christ.

9. *Finally, look for ways to ENJOY your child.* Though you may sometimes feel as if you are simply surviving your child's teenage years, focus on the things about your son or daughter that bring a smile (or even a smirk) to your face.

Again, putting these principles into practice will take some time and effort. But it will be well worth your while. You'll be following an important command from the Lord, and you'll be equipping your son or daughter for a strong relationship with Christ. Furthermore, you'll probably experience some personal spiritual growth. I almost always feel encouraged when I talk about God with my own daughters, and they're only two and three! Even the simplest of spiritual truths can change our attitudes and behaviors. The deeper questions and truths your child may be pursuing may cause you to dig into the Scriptures more than you ever have. What a great outgrowth of your spiritual parenting!

Be encouraged that, as parents, we won't be able to train up our sons and daughters perfectly. We need God's grace in this area of our lives as much as we do in every other area. We all need to rely on the Lord and trust that "love covers over a multitude of sins" (1 Peter 4:8), misunderstandings, and good intentions gone bad.

And take heart: You don't have to be a Bible scholar to teach your child! Do your best, and God will meet you more than halfway. If you don't know the answer to a specific question your child asks, let him or her know that when you have a chance, the two of you can look it up together.

The task of raising godly children *is* an awesome one, and I pray that your youth group will provide resources that will help you dialogue with your child about spiritual things. Such resources can facilitate a great partnership between youth ministers and families, both of whom want to train up righteous young people.

So You Want to Volunteer

Beyond using your resources to support a youth ministry and partnering with the ministry as you parent your child spiritually, some of you will sense a call to invest your time and yourself in week-to-week youth work.

Hooray for you! As a youth pastor I know that every person who volunteers and pours out God's love to students is a personal blessing to me. In this chapter I'll share with you the ways in which you can plug into and stay involved in youth ministry. Once again, I'd like to start things off with a real-life story about three men who sensed that God was pulling them into the always thrilling, sometimes chaotic world of youth work.

The Three Amigos

In June 1998 I had just finished a rigorous four years of study at Talbot Seminary and ministry at the First Evangelical Free Church of Fullerton.

Days after my seniors from First EV Free graduated, I donned cap and gown to receive my master of divinity degree. I was exhausted!

I had also courted Jerusha during the past year and proposed to her on Catalina Island. (It's a *great* story…ask me sometime!) In the midst of all this, I began the process of candidating at other churches.

I can't tell you how ready I was for a vacation by the time I accepted the position of Pastor of Student Ministries at Tri-Lakes Chapel (TLC) in Colorado. They asked me to begin work right away, but I opted to schedule a month off to recharge my energy, spend time with my fiancée before our September wedding, and prepare for the ministry adventure ahead.

When Thomas, a small-group leader for a group of TLC students, called me in July, I hadn't really said good-bye to my previous ministry, let alone thrown myself into the one before me. I felt relieved that he'd just left a message on my answering machine.

But Thomas was persistent enough to call me back, and this time he caught me at home. Unlike me, Thomas was "all systems go" with my new role in TLC's youth ministry, and he shot a barrage of questions at me about my plans, my philosophy of ministry, and my hopes for the youth at Tri-Lakes. I didn't *want* to be frustrated or annoyed with a potentially great guy calling me from my new home church, but I honestly was. I had heard that the first people on your doorstep when you begin a new ministry are usually those with an agenda or a gripe.

Still, after a brief conversation I assured him that I'd love to talk when I arrived in a couple of weeks. I hung up the phone and hoped for the best.

Days after I started work in Colorado, Thomas and his close friend, Doug, treated me to lunch. They chose Chevy's—a Mexican restaurant that reminded me of home—so I thought at the very least I'd get a good meal out of what could be a challenging meeting.

Guess what? The food turned out to be the *very least* of the blessings I received that day. Not only did these guys want to fully support the youth ministry, they wanted to be an encouragement to me personally. In fact, through the years I ministered at Tri-Lakes, these men not only became a life support for me, they became friends whom I cherish to this day.

Though neither of these guys volunteered that day to work with me on staff, I quickly saw their potential as youth leaders. These men and another good friend of theirs, Mark, had already been working with a small group of eighth graders, including their own sons. The boys respected their dads and thought it was "cool" to have the "Three Amigos" as their leaders.

Because the previous youth ministry hadn't had small groups, the Three Amigos had taken it upon themselves to meet a felt need by starting a Bible study of their own. When they found out that I planned to institute small groups across the board in the student ministry, they wanted to bring their youth discipleship group under the umbrella of TLC's youth ministry.

The Three Amigos turned out to be fantastic additions to my volunteer staff. They led their own group of young men with integrity, purpose, and commitment. In addition, they helped write lesson plans for other groups and occasionally taught during youth service. For two years all three men consistently poured themselves into the lives of the students in their small group. These guys were invaluable.

But at one point I lost Mark. Not because he didn't want to continue but because his son felt he might not grow as much spiritually with his dad as his discipleship leader. I have a rule that parents can volunteer as long as their son or daughter feels comfortable with the arrangement. Parents are always welcome to attend an event, but it may not be best for them to be a core-group leader, let alone their own child's leader.

Luke asked that his dad step down, and he did. But the Amigos group continued, and as the guys graduated, they honored all three of the men who had led them. This is how core groups work best: when they are led by committed, godly people with enough wisdom and patience to guide students in God's ways. I was proud to work with the Three Amigos, and I feel that way about all of my volunteers.

Before You Even Consider It

This may sound silly, but before you join a youth ministry as a volunteer (or even as a paid staff member), you must decide whether you really *like* young people. Though the goals of reaching the next generation with the gospel and helping disconnected youth find fulfillment in Christ are noble, alone they will not sustain you for the long haul of working with students.

Leaders who stay plugged into student ministries do so because God has given them a heart for young people. They don't just endure the craziness of all-night events or weeks at summer camp; they *enjoy* these times (at least most of the time). Leaders who last listen to the sometimes petty, sometimes amazingly profound conversations of young people because they *care about* the students they serve.

If you find that you become easily annoyed with adolescents or that you have no desire to enter their world and truly know them, *please* do not jump into youth ministry. God has certainly given everyone a heart for something, but becoming a Christian does not mean you will suddenly have a burning desire to work with kids between the ages of eleven and eighteen.

When my wife invited her small group of sophomore girls over to her parents' house, her mom overheard the dinner-table talk and asked Jerusha later, "How can you do it? Their conversation was so inane." The only way Jerusha could explain it was that she cared about the girls and what they were thinking.

Though Jerusha's mom ministered to twentysomethings for some time and served young children in Sunday school and Vacation Bible School, she could not imagine hanging out with students in between childhood and early adulthood. Adolescents were *not* her thing.

My counsel: Ask the Lord to reveal to you whether youth ministry is a good fit for you. Dialogue with Him. Listen to what He has to say to you through Scripture and the advice of others.

Perhaps you're thinking, *But the youth pastor didn't ask me to join the youth staff.* Youth leaders tend to be very busy. Most don't have time to recruit. Beyond that, they may not want to issue a "cattle call" for volunteers because they'd rather trust that *God* will call quality disciplers who will come on their own initiative.

There's no doubt that God longs for you to minister somewhere, but not everyone is meant to work with students. Please don't take this to mean that you can't help in some way! You can serve youth in many ways without volunteering on the youth-ministry staff. (See the previous chapter for some ideas.)

If you sense that the Lord has given you the go-ahead to volunteer, however, take the next step by visiting the youth program. If possible, attend a youth service, a Bible study, and a special event before making a final decision. Hopefully this will give you a feel for the style of ministry and your level of comfort with it.

Next, check to see that your schedule works with the student ministry schedule. A man recently approached me and expressed interest in a position on our team, but he had class every Wednesday night. Not only would he have missed half of our weekly program, he would have missed the small-group time, during which deeper connections are made. Obviously, this arrangement would not have worked.

Try mapping out on your calendar what a week (or a month if you're superambitious) in youth ministry would look like. This may help you determine if your schedule will allow you to invest in the lives of students. Being a youth leader takes time and commitment, not to mention energy and perseverance. If you're showing up only once a month or every now and then, you will not be able to build relationships necessary for Christlike leadership.

At our church I ask all volunteers to make a one-year commitment. I do this for two reasons: to encourage leaders to be people of their word and to call them to press through some of the challenges that may make them want to throw in the towel. I want the students I serve to have a consistent, loving influence. The ideal would be for every leader to make a six-year commitment (or seven if a youth group includes sixth graders), but I know that's impossible for many. One year *is* a rather hefty chunk of time to give as it is. Most volunteers who take the plunge, however, recognize they've barely scratched the surface with a group of students after twelve months.

Pledging a year may not be a requirement for youth-ministry volunteers at your church, but I exhort you to make a personal commitment along these lines. If it would help you, tell your youth pastor the amount of time you feel able to give and ask him to encourage you in following through with your personal commitment.

What Are You Getting Into?

It is virtually impossible for a youth pastor to get to know all of the students in his group as intimately as he needs to in order to lead them effectively. That's where volunteer leaders, people like you, come in.

Every youth pastor must balance the administrative, teaching, and counseling aspects of his ministry with the "hang out and get to know students" part. Even if a "superpastor" knew all the students by name and attended their piano recitals and football games, he would never be able to hear all their hurts or help them apply Scripture to various aspects of their lives.

This is especially true of large ministries. I currently work with several hundred students and rely on a team of fortysome volunteer staff members and five paid interns to reach these young men and women.

A youth ministry does not have to consist of a couple hundred or a hundred (or even twenty!) students to necessitate volunteers. In fact, the pressures can be immense for a youth leader who's expected to do it all himself, and your service may be a lifeline to a weary brother or sister.

Half of the students in a group may also feel that they can't *really* connect with a pastor or director because he or she is the opposite gender. A girl struggling with anorexia might not approach her male youth pastor, but she might confide in a female small-group leader (yes, even someone else's mom!). A guy who's mired in Internet pornography probably wouldn't want to meet with the female director of a youth ministry, but he might talk with a male adult leader (again, even if it's someone else's dad) who has consistently invested in this young man's life. In fact, sometimes what a young man or woman really *aches* to do is confess to his or her parent(s), but a student may feel paralyzed and terrified at that prospect. An adult volunteer, possibly someone else's mother or father, is safer and is also mature enough not to respond like a peer.

The cover letter I send to potential youth-ministry volunteers states that "a leader is responsible for knowing personally and discipling his or her core group. This discipling is done on a weekly basis.... Much of the discipling happens just by a leader befriending the students in his or her core group and modeling what it means to live the Christian life. However, leaders often [direct] their core groups in Bible study during [weekly] meetings."[3]

Some of you may have balked at that last statement: "direct...in Bible study." You may be thinking, *There's no way I could lead a group of fifteen-year-olds through the book of Revelation.* Don't worry; you're not alone. Most people couldn't do that!

You don't have to be an expert theologian or even a great Bible-study leader to guide a small group. In fact, the less able you feel, the more *Christ's* power will be at work, not your own. Remember Paul's declaration in 2 Corinthians 12:9: "[Christ's] power is made perfect in [our] weakness."

Either the youth pastor or a helpful clerk at your local Christian bookstore can help you find a manual on leading a small group as well as a number of Bible studies that include leaders' guides with suggestions for facilitating discussion, making applications to daily life, and so on.[4] With prayer and continued reliance on God's help, willing—if a bit fearful—servants like you and me can use these tools to lead small groups. Also, take a moment to look back at the "Outline of an Hour" section in chapter 2.

Bible study is not the *only* thing that happens during a discipleship-group meeting. If the Lord has given you the heart for youth work, He'll equip you with the skills you need as well. Your part is to just say yes when God asks you to do what's necessary for Him to equip you.

At our church we ask all leaders to attend at least one scheduled youth activity a month. You may want to ask if the youth ministry subsidizes the cost of individual events for leaders as this may determine which events you will be able or willing to attend.

We require our staff and volunteers to be present at monthly leaders' meetings as well. Churches have anywhere between zero and four staff meetings per month; find out what your particular ministry will require.

Finally, we affirm that while the commitment to become a youth-ministry volunteer is a serious one, it will *definitely* be worth the time and effort.

Before you read the following sections, I want to offer you some encouragement. A few of the things I describe may seem intimidating, if not downright terrifying. Please don't feel overwhelmed. What I present are just guidelines and hopes for leaders. You don't have to meet every criterion to be an excellent leader. Don't let self-doubt overpower your desire to serve. God is, and always will be, with you!

Expectations

Making it possible to have the level of ministry we aim for requires a certain mentality and lifestyle among leaders. Following is a rough estimate of the hourly commitments we ask our volunteer leaders to make:

- Sunday school: 1.5 hours
- Bible study/small group: 1.5 hours
- Staff meetings every other week: 1 hour
- I also hope that leaders will spend at least 10 hours per month connecting with students and parents through programmed activities (events, retreats, etc.) or personally initiated activities, such as praying for students, grabbing coffee, skating, surfing, or shopping with them.

I believe that to truly invest in students, these hours are minimal commitments when leaders are seeking to build lasting connections.

It would be great if every leader could meet one-on-one with each small-group participant. I know, however, that this is a tad unrealistic. Some students won't even *want* to meet with their leader, especially if they are hurting too deeply or know they're not investing in their relationship with the Lord. It's a lot easier to just hide a personal struggle or a sin issue in a group. And leaders do have *lives* outside of ministry! I really understand this; there aren't enough hours in my day to go to Starbucks or be on campus with all the students who need me.

Keep in mind that the amount of time a leader gives is not as important as his or her devotion. Consistency is of the utmost importance, since students will usually be as dedicated to Bible study and service as their leader is. Most young people won't take initiative, but they will often respond to the genuine interest of a leader.

Beyond the minimum time commitment expected of youth leaders, it's likely that a youth pastor will also encourage staff members to develop their own spiritual maturity as they oversee the spiritual growth of their core group. As leaders model a growing relationship with Christ, they give students a healthy, balanced example of consistent discipline, positive attitude and speech, faithfulness, and personal integrity.

Many youth pastors also call their leaders to a high standard of behavior, asking that they model Christlikeness in their entertainment choices and conversations and by the way they dress. I like how the ministry application for one church expresses this: "Vulgar or offensive language...or jesting that would [offend] other staff, students, or the Lord is not to be used."

At our church I also remind prospective leaders that they are accountable to God for their actions and choices. I will not be able to make sure every leader is honoring the Lord and modeling Christlikeness. However, as the pastor who is ultimately responsible for the students God has entrusted to me, I do request that leaders willingly make themselves accountable to my staff and to me.

Finally, keep in mind that there are no "sovereign states" in a youth ministry. If you want to be a leader, you need to be ready to join with other staff members in fulfilling the ministry vision.

Defining the Ministry

If you do not know how the youth pastor defines his vision, goals, or objectives, meet with him to discuss these matters.

For example, one of my goals is to have enough core-group leaders for a student-to-leader ratio of between six and eight to one. I say this to encourage you not to bite off more than you can chew. You may want to help everyone—that's wonderful! But you cannot have the kind of impact on twenty students that you can on six or eight.

You've probably seen in your own circle of friends that it's difficult to be close to several people at once. Conversation becomes a bit shallower or more difficult the larger a group gets. This isn't rocket science. As more personalities and opinions (not to mention more *mouths*) are added to the mix, there will be fewer opportunities for everyone to be heard and understood.

Even if your church has no set limits on group size, please consider keeping your group small enough so that true fellowship can occur. If you are pressured by the pastor or another leader to disciple more students, either explain as graciously as you can the reason for limiting your numbers or, better yet, recruit another adult to help you disciple the group.

Characteristics of a Leader

I have found the following list helpful for volunteer leaders. You may want to review each item and pray that God would reveal any weak areas in your life that you need Him to strengthen. *No one* will possess all of these traits. Yet it's important for leaders to commit their lives to acquiring and building them.

1. *Character and integrity.* Leaders should be able to say with the apostle Paul, "Follow my example, as I follow the example of Christ" (1 Corinthians 11:1). In every area of a leader's life— such as language, entertainment, dress, finances, relationships, and so on—commitment to God should be evident.

2. *Spiritual maturity.* The disciplines of prayer, Bible study, and worship (all of which we seek to teach and model for students) should be a consistent part of each leader's life.

3. *Reliability.* Faithful, dependable leaders inspire students (see Luke 16:10-11). Inconsistency calls into question even the greatest qualities of a leader.

4. *Positive self-image.* So many students struggle with a negative self-image and look to leaders for help. Therefore, leaders should understand that their worth comes from what Christ thinks of them. Leaders should also be careful not to seek the validation of students. Though we all want to be liked, compromising respect by playing for a student's approval will only backfire. Emotionally needy people rarely succeed as volunteer leaders. Good leaders are interested in the needs of their students, not merely their own needs.

5. *Clear vision.* Between the junior-high and college years, young people formulate many of their core beliefs and much of their lifelong character. Because they are malleable and open during these years, students need leaders who understand the importance of this time of life.

6. *Commitment to the youth ministry, to the greater church, and to the family.* Effective youth leaders support the vision and purpose of the entire church. In addition, good youth leaders not only communicate with families and support what godly parents teach at home, they also partner with parents in lovingly investing in students' lives. Good leaders never undercut (with words or actions) biblical family values.

7. *Commitment to authenticity.* Most students will automatically examine the life of their leader, and students can spot a fake miles away. Some parents aren't comfortable with being transparent with students, but for young people to grow into adult believers, they need to see salvation being worked out in the life of a more mature (not a pretending-to-be-perfect) Christian.

8. *A servant's heart.* Youth work is often a thankless job. Leaders seek neither praise nor recognition. Instead, they take the initiative to serve (see Romans 12:10-11; Matthew 20:25-28).

9. *Teachability.* A continued desire to grow as a leader—evident in attitude as well as in little things, such as faithful attendance at leaders' meetings—characterizes a good youth volunteer.

10. *Team player.* Leaders who work with others to achieve the overall goals of a youth ministry mutually edify and support one another. Undermining other volunteers or creating division between staff and/or students shouldn't occur in a healthy ministry. Christ teaches us to value unity and to work together (see Ephesians 4:3).

11. *Love expressed in action.* As 1 John 3:18 instructs, "Dear children, let us not love with words or tongue but with actions and in truth." Many students see only poor examples of parental love in action. Many don't see faith acted out in their homes. An effective leader is able to demonstrate Christ's love to students through action.

This list could intimidate any mature believer! Let me emphasize again: No leader will possess all of these traits. All leaders are imperfect and are working their faith out with "fear and trembling" (Philippians 2:12). You can avoid the perfection mentality by reminding yourself that He who called you to volunteer in a youth ministry is faithful to finish the good work He began in you (see Philippians 1:6).

A Look at Your Past

Whether or not your church requires you to disclose personal information, I would like to share the following checklist with you. I use it to get anyone who might be drawn to youth ministry to think about some important issues. Perhaps it will stir up your thoughts as well.

While experience with any of the following can have potentially negative effects on a leader and the students he or she shepherds, God can also use them in positive ways to change or strengthen His people. Such experiences can either prepare a person for working with youth or disqualify him or her. This depends largely upon an individual's commitment to and intimacy with the Lord as well as whether he or she was a willing participant or was forced to take part in these things. That is why I ask prospective volunteers to indicate whether they have had any prior involvement or experience with:

- divorce*
- alcohol abuse
- drug use

---

* I would like to clarify that divorce is certainly not viewed on the same level as witchcraft or drug abuse or any of the other extreme things on this checklist. An agonizing divorce, however, can certainly impact the way a man or woman deals with others, especially with those of the opposite sex. In addition, if the would-be volunteer had the heartbreaking experience as a child of seeing his or her parents go through a divorce, the revelation of this might become an *asset* for the youth ministry. Think of all the tenderness and understanding this person could offer a young person who is going through the fire of his or her parents' divorce.

- tobacco use
- homosexuality
- premarital sex
- sexual abuse
- physical abuse
- emotional abuse
- pornography or unhealthy sexual fantasizing (including the use of video games, magazines, phone, Internet, etc.)
- cults
- witchcraft
- legal difficulties (including an arrest or criminal record)
- eating disorders

In asking prospective leaders to reveal these things, it's not my desire to expose their sin or rip the skeletons out of their closets. Instead, I am seeking to protect the students I love from potentially unhealthy or predatory leaders.

A prospective volunteer will not be automatically disqualified from serving in the youth ministry if he or she has experienced any of these things. Many moms and dads who have struggled with some of these things have served on my staff. But time, faith, and, most often, counseling brought healing from past experiences for these mothers and fathers. By the time they came on board as youth-ministry volunteers, God had already brought them to a much healthier place.

This checklist allows me to address past issues by asking the person how long it's been since his or her last experience with the issue or how intense the feelings and behaviors currently are. Meeting with a prospective leader gives me a sense of whether the area of struggle may be ministry debilitating.

After a prospective volunteer evaluates him- or herself and decides to take the plunge, I recommend that the volunteer meet with me. (You would meet with whoever oversees the youth ministry at your church.)

Face to Face

When meeting with prospective volunteers for my youth staff, I start by asking, "What are the top two reasons you want to work with me?" (Their response to this question helps me steer away drill-sergeant types or "I have the answer for young people today" leaders.) I also attempt to find out what fears they have about youth ministry.

I've often been told that parents feel they're too old to work with students. I share with these moms and dads that young people will respond to the oldest person in the room who shows real love for them. Students don't need another peer; they need someone who models Christ authentically.

Some leaders fear that they don't have a strong enough relationship with the Lord. I tell them that they can lead only as far as they have traveled themselves. I ask them to describe what characterizes their walk with God. In some instances the Enemy has tried to trick potential leaders into believing that they aren't spiritually mature enough to disciple students. Sometimes, however, asking these questions helps me redirect those who want to experience the fun of youth ministry but have not yet established the solid personal and spiritual convictions it takes to serve young people.

I also ask prospective volunteers what their greatest struggle is and how they think it may impact their work with students. This is when I review any checked boxes from the Personal Information List. Again, my purpose is not to expose someone but to protect students. Youth pastors are *not* looking for perfect leaders; we're looking for those who know their own weaknesses and are pursuing healing and growth.

I discuss with prospective leaders what they were like as teenagers and what students they think they might minister to best. Youth ministries often contain various "tribes"—groups of students who express themselves in unique ways through dress, involvement in school, sports, drama, or music. A former "jock" may have trouble with a group of artsy students, and a leader who listens only to classical music may not connect with "Goth" or "Metal" kids. I try to help leaders who want to get involved find a niche with a tribe that's a good fit for their particular personality and background. Moreover, if a volunteer has experienced victory over a particular sin, I may be able to pair him or her up with a student who is facing the same struggle.

Finally, I ask prospective leaders about expectations. If they have unhealthy expectations of either me or themselves, I attempt to reveal these expectations and suggest a more balanced perspective.

Gentle Warnings

No matter what ministry you participate in, you will face times of both delight and dissatisfaction. Youth work is no exception. In fact, while physical exhaustion certainly comes with ministering to a group of toddlers, *emotional* frustration seems to spring up when working with junior-high and high-school students.

I'd like to prepare you for some of the challenges you may face in youth ministry:

1. *Disappointment.* The world around us screams for instant gratification and gauges success by how quickly results can be seen. Much of what leaders do with young people, however, is to plant and water seeds that will grow and bear fruit later in their lives. If you start with a long-haul perspective, you'll be better able to weather the teenage pattern of two steps forward, one (or three!) steps back without being disappointed either in them or in yourself.

2. *Spiritual dryness.* Ministering to anyone can be draining and can take time away from your personal relationship with Jesus. In John 4, Jesus promises to give unlimited refreshment to the thirsty. He refers to Himself as the Source of Living Water. Go to Him to be revitalized. Then, filled to overflowing, you will be able to serve out of an abundance rather than a deficit.

3. *Doubt.* Disappointment often leads to doubt. Youth leaders sometimes think that if they had just done something differently, a student would have made a good choice rather than a poor one. They wonder if they've made any impact at all in students' lives. This kind of doubt comes not from the Lord but from the Enemy. Leaders not only have limited ability to help, but we also make mistakes. There will be times you'll think you could have done something more. There are times when all of us miss an opportunity to show Christ's love. But always cling to God's assurance that the students you serve are in *His* care, not yours. Avoid the perfectionistic, must-do-everything-right mentality. As we all keep a humble, prayerful spirit, we can serve free of guilt and doubt.

How you handle the highs and the lows of youth ministry will determine whether you survive or thrive. You *will* make it, but I pray that you will make it with *joy!*

A Word in Closing

Parenting is not for the faint of heart, and neither is youth work. I pray I haven't scared prospective volunteers away! If you feel overwhelmed by the responsibilities and expectations discussed in this chapter but still feel drawn to minister to students, then you are in *exactly* the right place.

As we humbly ask the Lord for help, He will provide above and beyond what we can imagine, filling us with strength and skill, joy and dedication. I hope this chapter has inspired some of you to answer God's call to faithfully serve young people.

What Parents Like You Had to Say

From Todd, father of four kids between the ages of four and eighteen:

I always felt that the junior-high and high-school years were critical for our children's spiritual growth. I wanted them to connect with and stay connected to godly friends and mentors. I also felt that if I became involved with the student ministries on some level, I could participate in my kids' church experience, helping protect them and guide them through these tough years. It was extremely important to me, however, to give my kids the space they needed. I've enjoyed very open relationships with them, and I've been fortunate that they've wanted me around. But I've always made it clear that if my children ever felt uncomfortable with me serving in a particular role in the youth ministry, I would step out and help in another capacity. I also emphasized that my kids and I could evaluate my work with the youth group year by year, in case their feelings were to change. So far I've been in youth ministry for two and a half years, and I love the opportunities it affords me to get to know my kids' friends as well as to see my children in different ways. Most important, I am able to do what God has called me to do: serve Him. Partnering with the youth group has been a great experience for me.

From a mother of three, one in high school, one in junior high, and one in elementary school:

When I was growing up, a group of godly adults invested their lives in me. These six women were there not only for me but for my peers as well. They continually brought the Word of God before us and helped us apply the Scripture to our lives. They exuded the love of the Lord. They modeled the Christian life before us and showed us how to be godly wives and mothers. I believe that their faithful influence played a major part in my staying on the narrow path.

I decided to thank God for His grace in providing these women for me by serving others in the same way. That's why I'm involved as a core-group leader at my church. My husband also leads a small group. We both believe that it's important to work with youth because they can really make their faith their own once they reach junior high. At this point it's critical that young men and women begin to own their walk with the Lord, their journey with Him. We want to show young people they can live a life that honors God no matter how old (or young, as the case may be) they are. By God's grace I have no skeletons in my closet. I say this not in a prideful way, but to encourage parents out there—your son or daughter *can* stay faithful to God in this time of temptation. I'm always asking God the question, "How can I help students make the right choices?" In His mercy He not only answers me but equips me. This benefits young people and, by extension, my family. My own children are coming of age, and serving in the youth ministry allows me to live out a life of service before them. What a gift from God that is!

Six

Praying for a
Youth Ministry

JOHN WESLEY ONCE claimed, "God does nothing but in answer to prayer."

That statement sort of scares me. I think about the times I've started an event and forgotten to pray. I think about the Sundays I get up to preach, and though I tried to talk with the Lord beforehand, my prayers seemed weak and pointless.

And then I remember that God responds not only to *my* prayers but to the faithful intercession of the leaders, students, and families who make up the youth ministry. (By the way, *intercession* is a fancy word that means "prayer for others." You will notice that throughout this chapter I use this noun as well as the verb *intercede,* which means "prayer that is offered on behalf of others.") Most important, the Lord answers Christ Himself who "is at the right hand of God and is also interceding for us [youth ministers]" (Romans 8:34).

Thank God that I am not alone in prayer. Thank God for those who gather together to pray for the leaders of their churches and their youth groups. Thank God that He *does things* in response to these prayers.

When Jerusha and I came to candidate at Emmanuel Faith Community Church, we had a few minutes to spare before one of our interviews. Someone had told me that it would be a good idea to talk to a neighbor of the church and find out what kind of reputation it had.

So I knocked on the door of a home across the street from the church's sanctuary. No answer. Undaunted, I tried knocking on the door of a welcoming-looking house adjacent to the athletic field.

I heard a voice call "Coming!" and after a few moments, a tall woman answered the door, flanked by her two sons and a daughter. I introduced myself and asked my question, but I could not have been less prepared for her response.

"So *you're* the candidate. My name is Sherrie, and I've been working with the high-schoolers for a while. In fact, a group meets here on Tuesdays to pray for the ministry."

I had to laugh. We chatted for a few minutes, but since Jerusha had stayed in the car (twelve weeks into her pregnancy, she didn't feel so hot), I started to wind down our conversation.

Sherrie and her kids walked me to the car and introduced themselves to my wife. Jerusha got a kick out of God's amazing timing and guidance and enjoyed a brief conversation with Sherrie.

When we arrived at EFCC to start work, not only did Sherrie continue praying, but she encouraged Jerusha and me with thoughtful notes as well. The Jacksons helped after Jasmine was born (Sherrie makes a killer dish of sour-cream chicken and a dynamite pan of corn bread), and Sherrie faithfully led in the high-school ministry.

My wife and Sherrie also codiscipled a group of girls, and Jerusha knew that Sherrie's prayers made a difference in the youth group.

Why Pray?

First and foremost, we pray because God commands us to pray. Throughout the Scriptures, the Lord exhorts us to worship Him and intercede for others in prayer. Ephesians 6:18 makes this clear: "Pray in the Spirit on *all occasions* with all kinds of prayers and requests. With this in mind, be alert and always keep on praying for all the saints" (emphasis added).

Prayer is the most specific, practical thing we can do for a youth ministry and for our own children. It is not the last resort, but the first thing and really the best thing we can do. We also pray because God *does* answer. Elijah prayed believing that it made a difference, and it did (see 1 Kings 17:1–18:45). Moses believed that he might change God's mind because of His unchanging love (see Exodus 32:14). The people of Nineveh prayed because they believed God would show mercy if they repented, and He did (see Jonah 3:10). James 5:16 teaches that "the prayer of a righteous man is powerful and *effective*" (emphasis added). We pray because prayer changes things.

And we pray because it takes us into more intimate communion with God. "Prayer catapults us onto the frontier of the spiritual life.... It is the Discipline of prayer…that brings us into the deepest and highest work of the human spirit. Real prayer is life creating and life changing."[1]

If you want to see a youth ministry truly grow, really reach your child and many others and make a life-changing difference for eternity, start praying. Pray for your son's or daughter's experience in youth group. Pray for other students and the leaders. Pray for the vision to be carried out and for the upcoming events. Pray believing that God does things in response to prayer.

WHEN DO I PRAY?

The Word of God graciously instructs us how and when to pray. Let's deal first with when to intercede.

An oft-quoted verse on prayer found in 1 Thessalonians 5:17—"pray continually" (or in other translations, "pray without ceasing")—sometimes overwhelms those who intend to start praying. They haven't even begun to pray a little, let alone all the time.

This verse should encourage us, not frighten us. We can "pray continually" or "pray without ceasing" because God enables us to do so. He never gives a command that He cannot or will not equip us to obey.

You have many opportunities to "pray without ceasing" throughout your day. You can pray while you stand in line or sit in traffic. You can pray when you're on hold or waiting for a client or a colleague. You can pray in and through the ordinary and everyday things of life—washing dishes, doing laundry, having lunch at the office. While you will not spend all of this time in prayer for your child and his or her involvement in the youth group, you may choose to set aside a few moments to lift up the ministers and programs at your church.

The Bible does not require that we pray at certain times of day. Yet some churches teach that certain times are better to pray than others. This just isn't true. Psalm 5:3, Psalm 88:13, and Mark 1:35 all teach us to pray early in the morning. Psalm 63:6 and 119:148 encourage us to meditate on the Lord "through the watches of the night." First Thessalonians 3:10 records that Paul prayed both "night and day." We, too, can pray at any time and, therefore, in any place.

If you ask God to lay the youth ministry on your heart throughout the day or week, He will do so. He wants people to pray that pastors and leaders, students and families would fulfill His purposes and be fulfilled in them.

Often, when people ask me, "When should I pray?" I encourage them to get to know themselves. If you're more alert at a certain time of day, use that time to pray. If you feel harried and harassed in the morning, don't force yourself to pray. Let God lead you. He intended prayer to be a joy, not an obligation. Prayer is supposed to be delightful conversation with God, who calls Himself our Friend and our Abba (Greek for "Daddy").

If it would work better for you to have a time set aside to pray specifically for the youth ministry, you can certainly schedule something. Perhaps you'd like to pray with others to minimize distraction. Whatever way God best moves through you, go with it. Don't try to box yourself in to one "right" way to pray. You can intercede for the youth ministry in an infinite number of ways and at any time that presents itself.

Don't Get Discouraged

People sometimes hear about great men and women of faith who seemed to live out the "pray continually" passage of Scripture. John Wesley reportedly spent two hours every day in prayer; Martin Luther devoted three hours a day to the discipline. Adoniram Judson withdrew seven times a day to engage in what he called "the holy work of prayer."

I don't know about you, but testimonies like this daunt me. Yet as Richard Foster points out, "Many of us…are discouraged rather than challenged by such examples. Those 'giants of faith' are so beyond anything we have experienced that we are tempted to despair. But rather than flagellating ourselves for our obvious lack, we should remember God always meets us where we are and slowly moves us along into deeper things."[2]

Let me emphasize this: You do not have to be perfect to start praying. As Foster mentioned, God meets us right where we are. If the only prayer you can come up with is, "God please bless the youth ministry," you can rejoice that He moved through you. This prayer is important to God, as are all prayers.

The motives of our hearts matter more to God than the eloquence of our words. The quality (meaning the purity and intention) of our prayers rather than the quantity counts most with the Lord.

Let us not fall into guilt, which comes from the Evil One. He would like us to believe that our prayers are not enough, that we can't make a difference unless we spend the night interceding, or at least an hour once a week. This is a horrible lie.

God not only meets us where we are, He is the One who enables us to pray in the first place. Be not discouraged, but encouraged! The fact that you are even reading this chapter shows that you want to pray for the ministry and for your child. You've taken the first step with God, and He will walk with you as you intercede for the youth group.

"Lord, Teach Us to Pray"

Real prayer is something we learn. Luke records a disciple asking Christ to instruct him and the other disciples in the ways of prayer (see Luke 11:1).

Like the disciples, we need to learn to pray. In the process of being taught to pray, we will question and doubt, we will experiment, and we will even fail. That's okay. In fact, I'd say that's *great!* You truly learn something when you've explored it in all kinds of ways, possibly all the way from exhilarating success to fall-on-your-face failure.

We can be instructed in the ways of prayer by reading Scripture. Great resources such as concordances and Bible dictionaries can lead you to passages on prayer in the Scriptures. In fact, while researching for this chapter, I used the NIV concordance often, thanking God as I did that He did not leave me in the dark trying to remember where I'd read or heard something about prayer.

We also learn about prayer by praying. That may sound somewhat circular, but it is nonetheless true and essential. We cannot wait to pray until we've "learned everything." Like the disciple in Luke 11:1, we need to ask that Christ would teach us to pray. And as we practice, we learn more about this holy work, this discipline of prayer.

By seeking out and observing those who know how to pray, we grow even more. Jesus Himself provides the perfect example of a life lived in prayer. He prayed for others, for Himself, and in worshiping the Father. As we follow Christ's lead, we can pray in the same ways He did.

Other biblical figures teach us about prayer as well. I mentioned Moses, Elijah, and Jonah before, but there are countless others: Hannah, Esther, the disciples, and the apostles, for starters. Each of the prayerful men and women of the Bible instruct us in different methods of prayer.

In addition, we can find guidance and direction from faithful believers down through the ages. Through their writings, these great men and women of faith teach us. Richard Foster quotes many of these in his book

Prayer: Finding the Heart's True Home. I don't think I could have written this chapter without Foster's insights and examples as well as his remarkable work in gathering the teachings of past masters.

Men and women of God who influence our daily walk can also teach us to pray. I remember watching and learning from Phil Howard, my childhood pastor. His prayers and teaching on prayer continue to shape me today. My mother and father also guided me in the practice of prayer. Even my precious daughters remind me to come to God "like a little child" (Mark 10:15).

In order to pray effectively for your child and for a youth ministry, you may want to observe or pray with someone who knows how to intercede for pastors or leaders. You may also learn to pray by asking for specific prayer requests from the youth workers. In this way, you will be better equipped to pray.

Again, we do not have to have it all together before we pray. It's as we pray, as we test the waters, that we learn and grow. And through the other means I just mentioned, we can grow deeper roots in the practice of prayer.

APPROACH THE THRONE OF GRACE WITH CONFIDENCE

We sometimes feel unsure in prayer because we don't know if what we want to pray for is "right" or "good." Yet God tells us in Hebrews 4:16 to "approach the throne of grace with confidence." How can we do this?

Some people have learned to pray by adding the words "if it be Your will" to almost every request they make. Yet Jesus never interceded for another person in this way. Neither did the apostles or prophets.

Richard Foster explains,

They obviously believed that they knew what the will of God was before they prayed the prayer of faith. They were so immersed in the milieu of the Holy Spirit that when they encountered a specific situation, they knew what should be done...there was evidently no room for indecisive, tentative, half-hoping...prayers.[3]

We don't have to wonder if it's God's will that students come to know Christ, that teachers and small-group leaders disciple successfully, or that the ministry carry out the purposes of God. We can pray these things (and others like them) with confidence, for we know that God wills that His children know Him, grow in Him, and lead others in His ways.

In addition, no one needs to worry about having too little faith to pray. Where we lack faith, God is faithful (see 2 Timothy 2:13). When we are weak, He is strong (see 2 Corinthians 12:9). If we humble ourselves to confess that we don't believe and that we cannot believe without Him, He will meet us and guide us graciously.

A dear friend—Blair—teaches students to pray. After meeting with a group of mothers who felt disappointed in the shallow prayers of their children, she felt God prompting her to model for others how to pray. She asked the moms, "How can our kids pray when no one is teaching them or modeling for them *how* to pray?"

Last year Blair mentored a group of high-school students, and the results were powerful. Her students began to pray for themselves and those in the high-school ministry. As God answered their prayers, they matured in faith. The testimonies of these young men and women then cultivated in other students a desire to pray.

In addition, these students learned important lessons about prayer. The following "Blairism" impacted students and stuck with me as well: "Surrender with legs." In prayer we do not surrender, lying down weakly, as if defeated. Rather, we surrender before the throne of grace with confidence. We surrender with legs, prepared for action.

Blair also taught her students about the four levels of prayer. First, we pray *wishing*. Then we pray *hoping*. Then, as we grow in confidence, we pray *believing*. And finally, we pray *overcoming*.

We cannot begin to pray with confidence unless we learn to do so. "Wishing prayers" are the beginning. Somewhat akin to throwing a coin in a fountain, wishing prayers reflect our dream that prayer might change something. As we continue wishing, we sense that we've moved into *hoping*. Perhaps we've seen some prayers answered. Confidence grows with each new evidence of God's work.

Believing comes next. In believing prayer, we trust that God will do *something* when we pray, even if we don't always comprehend why He answers our prayers the way He does.

Ultimately, we *overcome*. At this point we trust God's work, and we know that His will is perfect. We boldly come to Him, triumphing over our fear and trepidation. Just because we've reached the believing or even the overcoming stage, however, does not mean we'll never again offer wishing or hoping prayers. We may pray on any or all of these levels throughout a lifetime of prayer or even in one specific prayer request.

Our hope lies in the fact that Christ "always lives to intercede for" those who approach God through Him (Hebrews 7:25).

Furthermore, others may believe or overcome for us when all we're able to do is wish or hope. We bear one another's burdens in prayer (see Galatians 6:2), standing in the gap when our friends and loved ones may be weak (see Ezekiel 22:30). You may be able to approach the throne of grace with confidence for someone else when you cannot do it yourself.

Mothers, fathers, grandparents, and siblings can believe and triumph with youth pastors and leaders. Boldly approaching God's throne together, families in youth ministry can make eternal changes.

How Do I Pray?

In general, prayer is not as complicated as we make it. We do not have to have the "right" words. Remember, our intention, not our eloquence, counts most to God. We do not need to edit our prayers. He loves our open, honest, and transparent requests. Besides, he already knows what is really in our hearts!

We don't have to follow certain forms of prayer, though methods such as the ACTS model (adoration, confession, thanksgiving, and supplication, which means "requesting") may guide us. We can pray in as many ways at as many times and in as many places as we can.

For example, Frank Laubach refers to "flash prayers," short prayers lifted to the Lord as quickly as they come to mind. Some people call similar prayers "arrow prayers."

In his book *Prayer: Finding the Heart's True Home,* Richard Foster writes about "breath prayers," which resemble flash or arrow prayers. Like flash or arrow prayers, breath prayers may be silent, or they may involve speaking one or two words. Marsha, one of my wife's mentors, uses this method (particularly when she's tired) and simply breathes someone's name and one word that encapsulates a request on that person's behalf.

Breath prayers can also be used in more formal or even liturgical ways. One example is the ancient Jesus prayer, the most famous of breath prayers: "Lord Jesus Christ, Son of God, have mercy on me, a sinner." Foster also gives examples of various breath prayers in his book and encourages his readers to discover their own individual breath prayers.[4]

Brother Lawrence, author of the Christian classic *The Practice of the Presence of God,* an excellent resource on many aspects of a daily relationship with Jesus, says that prayer is a lifting of the head and heart to heaven.

Prayer does not have to be formulaic or traditional. We don't have to pray with certain words or in a specific way to receive God's attention and favor.

Praying straight from Scripture can be absolutely life changing. In praying God's truths and promises back to Him, we trust Him more and pray within His will. Books such as the Praying the Bible series by WaterBrook Press, *The Power of a Praying Parent,* and *Prayer Changes Teens* guide you with specific Scriptures to pray for your child and for his or her leaders.

Another way to pray that you may want to explore is called "prayer-walking." You could stroll around your neighborhood, praying for the people on your block. You could walk through your own house, praying over each room. And you could certainly prayerwalk around the buildings on your church property. If you'd like to learn more about this method of prayer, read Janet Holm McHenry's excellent book *Prayer Walk*.

If you enjoy making lists, you might want to incorporate this practice into your prayer life. A mother I know who is an avid list maker set up a board on which she posted prayer lists for each day of the week. She also placed on the board pictures of the people for whom she prays. While she walks on her treadmill, she prays not only for her family and friends but also for the youth ministry. My picture and the pictures of several of my staff and volunteer leaders made it onto her prayer board.

You can pick up a calendar from the youth-ministry office and pray over each event. Or you can ask the youth pastor or your son's or daughter's small-group leader for a list of requests and needs. You don't even have to know the names of students in order to pray for them. The pastor or leader can give you the information you need (perhaps the gender of the person making the request and the general situation). God knows the names and all the details.

Believers can pray alone or corporately. Like Sherrie and Blair, you may wish to pray with others for your child and the youth ministry. Or maybe you would rather spend time alone. Either way, God delights in your willingness to pray for His leaders and for young people.

Incorporating pictures, music, or other symbols into your prayer time might be effective as well. You might want to get photos of the youth staff or students and pray with their faces in mind. Or you could use some meaningful worship songs as prayers.

Christians may pray silently. This kind of prayer, sometimes called contemplative prayer, takes a lot of practice and discipline. We are not used to silence, and it often frightens us to quiet our minds. Yet the Lord commands us to "be still, and know that I am God" (Psalm 46:10). As Christians mature, they often long for silence in God's presence.

Silent prayer often takes the form of listening. Sören Kierkegaard once said, "A man prayed, and at first he thought that prayer was talking. But he became more and more quiet until in the end he realized that prayer is 'listening.' "[5] Prayer is a conversation between God and His children. And conversations are not fulfilling unless both parties speak and listen.

As you intercede for your child and the youth ministry, try these different ways of praying and even some different postures. You may want to bow your head or lift your hands to heaven. You may feel led to kneel, or you may feel so overwhelmed that you fall prostrate before the Lord—interestingly, this is the most common prayer posture in the Bible.

I've said this several times, but remember: No "right" way to pray exists.

Finally, you can pray *specifically*. Allow me to identify a few specific prayer needs that apply to every ministry. You may notice that most of these needs apply to *both* students and leaders. Please keep in mind that these needs are *not* listed in order of importance.

You can intercede for...

- traveling mercies, physical safety, and stamina during every activity
- godly friends and mentors as well as healthy family relationships
- disciplined study for the pastor, for Bible-study facilitators, and for students
- money—that students in need would be able to attend youth-group events, that the ministry would have the resources it needs to function best, and so on.
- music—The psalms exhort us again and again to sing praises to the Lord. And teenagers need to connect with God-honoring music.

- appropriate boundaries, especially as students try to resist temptation and peer pressure to experiment with all kinds of impurity
- the clothes students wear—Pray especially for modesty, but also regarding piercings, tattoos, and certain looks that might lead students or leaders astray.
- addictions—Along with substance abuse, pray for those involved in the youth ministry who may have other addictions. A youth-pastor friend of mine just confided in me that he didn't know how to address some leaders who seemed addicted to overeating. Students may also suffer from problems with eating disorders, cutting, or others forms of self-injury.
- discernment for youth leaders, even about the minutest details of the ministry
- overburdened youth workers—that they would ask for help when it's needed. Prayers against stress and burnout are also very much appreciated!
- that students and leaders would live exemplary lives (see 1 Timothy 3:1-13 for specific things to pray for pastors in this area)
- the language used within the group (*Note:* Did you know there is a Cuss Control Academy? Seriously. It's in Chicago. Yet cussing isn't the only thing we need to pray about. Sarcasm, using the Lord's name in vain, and other demeaning and hurtful talk need prayer. You can pray that any unwholesome words would sound ugly to the students and that they would be convicted of sin in this area.)
- goals, vision, purpose
- a commitment of students and leaders to outreach as well as good relationships with those who do not know Christ
- that students would stay connected to the youth ministry

Think It Over

On behalf of my staff and many other youth-ministry teams, thank you for reading this chapter on prayer. I think it's the most important chapter in this book. Prayer changes things. Prayer makes a difference.

In closing I'd like to encourage you to periodically examine your prayers for your children and the youth ministry. The prayers you pray for others may point out needs of your own. Be alert to what God might be teaching you through your prayers.

Also, consider these pointed words from the book of James: "You ask and do not receive, because you ask with wrong motives, so that you may spend it on you pleasures" (4:3, NASB).

In *Celebration of Discipline,* Richard Foster writes, "To ask 'rightly' involves transformed passions, total renewal. In prayer, real prayer, we begin to think God's thoughts after Him…. Progressively we are taught to see things from His point of view."[6]

You may not always *want* to pray God's will. Perhaps you want to see something specific happen in a ministry because it's your passion that things be done this way or in that time frame. Or maybe you want to protect those you love *from* God's will, especially His sometimes-painful working in their lives.

I love the metaphor Janet Holm McHenry shared in *Prayer Changes Teens.* She sensed in praying for her son and daughter that she needed to "close the umbrella." For too long she had been trying to shelter kids from what God might want to do in their lives. But she could not control His will, particularly if He needed to discipline her children. In surrendering her passions to the Lord, McHenry found freedom and peace, and her kids were drawn closer to Jesus.[7]

Consider whether you are thinking God's thoughts after Him, as scientist Johann Kepler once said, or asking God to think your thoughts after you.

You may have noticed that praying for a youth ministry will probably require something of you. It will most likely take some effort on your part to learn how to pray, to find the ways and times that work best for you. It may take some patience to wait for God to answer. And true prayer may uncover some things within yourself that you'd rather not face.

Please don't be afraid of the work of prayer, for sweet fruit results from the toil. Intercession might even become so fulfilling that it distracts you from daily stresses and tasks. What a wonderful state that would be! Though prayer requires something of you, the returns far exceed the costs.

Finally, let me offer you this amazing encouragement. In John 15:7, Jesus tells us, "If you remain in me and my words remain in you, ask whatever you wish, and it will be given you." As we trust in Christ and His words, we may ask whatever we wish, for what we desire will be in line with His will. Then—and this absolutely astounds me—it will be given to us!

May we all pray for the ministry to youth in this spirit.

What Parents Like You Had to Say

From Keith, whose son Zach has participated regularly in high-school-ministry prayer meetings:

God has allowed me to pray over and for various ministries. As our sons got older, I partnered with the youth ministry and interceded on behalf of leaders, speakers, and students. I prayed specifically about events and prayed with other adults for things they observed or hoped for as a result of their participation with the youth ministry. Often in our involvement with Campus Crusade for Christ's Student Venture, we have hosted activities at our home and have participated in high-school campus outreach ministries. Before, during, and after these events, much of the focus has been on prayer for everyone involved. I saw that prayer changed me and things around me.

I've also seen prayer within a student ministry change my son. When he expressed that he wanted to see growth in his prayer life, I encouraged him to pursue those things that would help him develop a more intimate relationship of prayer with the Lord. He found that leaders and students from the high-school ministry would pray before small-group Bible study, and he decided to serve on this prayer team. I could sense an immediate change in my son when he'd come home from prayer. His attitude and behavior, his willingness to obey, and his focus on the things of God astounded me. In participating in this youth-ministry prayer group, my son has been trained by listening to others who know how to pray. He's also opened himself up to accountability, since those with whom he's prayed know him and follow up with him. Prayer for and with the student ministries at our church has meant a great deal to my family.

From Thomas, father of five, three in high school and two graduates:

The basic lesson I've learned is that prayer for youth workers is the most important thing I, as a parent, can do. If I really want youth leaders to effectively minister to my children and to the other students in the youth group, I need to pray for and with the youth staff and volunteers.

I recently had to learn this lesson the hard way. When the youth pastor at our church resigned after only one year, a close friend asked me if I had prayed intentionally and consistently for this pastor. I admitted that I had not, and I wondered if the circumstances might not have been different if our church (me included) had faithfully interceded for this young man.

I then had a wonderful experience shortly before our new youth pastor accepted the position at our church. In a dream God asked me to pray five things for the new youth minister. These five things had been illuminated by author and pastor J. I. Packer in an article on revival and refreshment that I'd read. I prayed for a powerful awareness of God's presence, daily vitality in God's Word, a deep sensitivity to sin—an awareness and sensitivity that would call this pastor to repentance and dependence on the work of Christ—strong unity with others, and fruitfulness in personal ministry. The dream I had was so vivid, so visceral, that I awoke feeling absolutely

certain that God had called me to be a devoted prayer sup-
porter for our new youth pastor and his ministry. Not only
has the Lord given me the responsibility to pray and joy in
prayer, He has also given me the words to use. I've learned
that you don't have to come up with the "right" things to pray
for a youth-group pastor. Interceding on behalf of a student
ministry is simply a matter of following the Holy Spirit and
staying committed to pray.

Seven

Dealing with Disappointment

In *THE PRINCESS BRIDE,* the Dread Pirate Roberts tells Princess Buttercup, "Life is pain, Highness. Anyone who tells you differently is selling something."

Life will disappoint you at one time or another. People will fail you. Ministries will fall short of your hopes and expectations. I wish I could tell you otherwise, but if I did, I'd be selling you a happily-ever-after fairy tale that could never come true.

For Christians, however, a promise of lifelong disappointment is not the end of the story. In John 16:33, Jesus proclaimed, "In this world you will have trouble. But take heart! I have overcome the world."

In Christ we can face disappointments, frustrations, and discontentment because we know that He retains control of every situation. His sovereignty and overcoming power allow us to trust that no matter what trouble comes our way, hope and peace await us in His embrace.

I've no doubt that you've heard words like these before. But I've also no doubt that, for all of us, hearing them again is important—*essential,* really—as we look at dealing with disappointment.

In previous chapters I've emphasized that youth leaders are imperfect. The same goes for youth groups; every student ministry will have flaws. Youth pastors and leaders will make mistakes. No youth group can live up to every one of your expectations, let alone God's standard of perfection.

So what can you do with feelings of dissatisfaction and distress about the youth ministry at your church?

The Bible provides some great tools for dealing with disappointment and directs us in how to approach those with whom we feel discontented. I'd like to take you through some of the different types of disappointment you may face while your child participates in a youth ministry.

Because disappointment can be so multifaceted, it's sometimes difficult to discern what we're truly feeling. Dissatisfaction can crop up over a single event or a temporary situation. While this disappointment certainly stings, we can usually deal with it fairly easily.

Sometimes, however, discontentment strikes a more powerful chord—a deep concern that a pattern may develop or a circumstance may never change. This level of disappointment will likely require both time and discernment to overcome.

Duffy Robbins, a youth-ministry leader, divides disappointment into four categories: facts, methods, goals, and values. He claims that disagreements over facts and methods can be solved somewhat readily, since changes necessary to suit both parties can usually be found. Robbins goes on to say that dissatisfaction with goals and values creates conflict and requires more patience, discernment, and compromise to overcome. According to Robbins, you cannot have discontentment with values without having frustration with goals.[1]

For our purposes in this chapter, I'd like to look at *limited disappointment*—usually resulting from disagreement over facts regarding a single issue and sometimes a disagreement over methods—and *expanded disappointment*—sometimes a disagreement over methods, but most often a disagreement over the goals and values of a youth ministry. In addition to these types of disappointment, we'll look at *overall disappointment* in which dissatisfaction extends to the structure and vision of the entire church.

You've Got Mail

Dear Miss Smith:

Please forgive us for writing this letter to you anonymously. Our daughter confided in us, and we do not want to lose her trust, so we figure anonymity was the safest route to take.

Our daughter attends the youth group and was one of the girls in your…core group. She shared just a little bit about your last evening with the girls, about why you were quitting being a core-group leader. We, as her parents, wanted to let you know that we are very unhappy with the manner in which you left. As a mature Christian woman, instead of negatively "sharing" with the girls, you needed to go to [the pastor].…

Please consider that if you have a group of ladies, there will always be some, whether it be one or twenty, who will have an "attitude" or a problem with church, no matter what church or youth group it may be. When these girls hear an adult verify their feelings of dissatisfaction, rebellion, etc., that just reinforces whatever negativity the girls may have and makes them feel like those feelings must be all right. They may then continue to nurture those feelings instead of overcoming them and maturing in the Lord. So, in the short and long run, that adult has done much more harm than good.

That is what we feel you may have done to some of the girls. Please consider going to the youth pastor personally, sharing with him your feelings, and then either going to the girls as a group and apologizing to them for exiting in the wrong way, or write them a note of apology. We feel this is the mature Christian thing to do and may go a long way in helping the girls with their negative attitudes. We are very concerned and ask you to prayerfully consider the contents and suggestions of this letter.

Sincerely,

A Concerned Mom and Dad

A good friend shared this note with me. It had been sent to one of the adult leaders in his ministry, and I thought it was a fabulous example of how mothers and fathers might handle *limited disappointment.*

These concerned parents dealt with a single instance. A youth leader made what these parents believed were some poor choices, and they felt disappointed.

What I call limited disappointment crops up when a specific occurrence or a short-term situation irks or offends us. Limited disappointment certainly feels frustrating, but because of its limited scope, we can usually face it and resolve it more quickly and easily than we can more complex levels of disappointment that might involve repeated offenses or a long-standing problem.

When you feel disappointed with a specific situation, the first step is to *evaluate how severe your dissatisfaction is.* Sometimes, if you merely stop and calm down a bit—perhaps even take a night to sleep on it—things may not appear as bad as they did at first. Ask yourself if your level of frustration matches the circumstances, or do you think you may be making more of the event than is warranted.

Should you determine after some consideration that your frustration necessitates confrontation, *go straight to the person with whom you're disappointed.* Notice that the "concerned parents" did not write to other moms and dads in their daughter's core group or to the senior pastor, or even to the youth pastor. They wrote directly to the offending party.

I commend these parents for addressing this problem directly, but let me add a word of caution about writing anonymous letters. Written communication can often be misunderstood, and it can upset a person who feels that he or she didn't have a chance to respond, let alone know who to respond to. Sometimes, however, a letter is the only option. Since Miss Smith left the church as well as the youth ministry, this mom and dad felt that their only recourse was to write to their daughter's former leader.

I would recommend that, as far as possible, parents follow the biblical pattern of confrontation as laid out in Matthew 18:15-17. The Bible instructs us to take our concerns directly to the person who has disappointed or sinned against us. Should that person reject initial exhortation, we are told to take one or two others with us. So at that point, you are to bring in another person, perhaps your spouse or a pastor or elder. If this second attempt to reach the offender should fail, the issue can be taken to the greater church body.

Most of the time, with temporarily disappointing situations, church-wide review and discipline will be unnecessary. Some single-event sin issues, however, may require immediate confrontation involving more than one person, perhaps the entire church. For example, any instance of abuse—whether physical, emotional, or sexual—that occurs during a youth event should be brought to the attention of the pastoral staff member who oversees that area, and it should probably be reported to the police or other authorities.

The Word of God does remind us, however, that regardless of the response of the offending party or the gravity of the central issue, Christians must "seek peace and pursue it" (Psalm 34:14). The goal is not to spread discontent but to seek resolution and peace. Furthermore, believers should always "know the whole truth and tell it in love" (Ephesians 4:15, MSG).

Make sure you have your facts straight and approach a person with Christlike grace. This does not mean that you beat around the bush or sugarcoat the truth. (Take note of the pointed but respectful words in the letter from the concerned mom and dad.) Loving words of truth may still pierce a person's heart. Yet the Bible says, "Faithful are the wounds of a friend" (Proverbs 27:6, KJV) who speaks "the truth in love" (Ephesians 4:15).

In some cases you may want to discuss the situation with someone who knows more about the ministry but isn't likely to gossip about it. Ask candid questions that might help clarify your understanding of the situation. After talking things over, you may find that your disappointment has been resolved and feel it's unnecessary to confront the person after all.

With the freedom to speak honestly with others comes the responsibility to do so with grace. I love the way Eugene Peterson translates Galatians 5:15: "If you bite and ravage each other, watch out—in no time at all you will be annihilating each other, and where will your precious freedom be then?" (MSG).

If you feel unable to speak the truth in love and to pursue peace rather than inciting conflict, *wait until you sense God has prepared your heart.* Though it may take some time, and the situation may be long past, faithfully restraining yourself until you can speak truth in love will please God.

Remember that your children are watching how you live. Many times they imitate what you do without asking why or how you did it. You can teach them biblical ways of dealing with disappointment so that they will see Christ in your example. What a privilege that is!

When I worked in Colorado, many of our students enjoyed paintballing. My high-school director planned several paintball outings, and I joined the students a couple of times during my four years at TLC. A church elder came with us, too, donning camouflage and all.

But every time I held a parents' meeting, one mom and dad would raise their hands during the Q&A portion and express reservations about the ethics of paintballing. From their perspective, such activities encouraged violence and taught students the wrong way to have fun.

I respected these parents and had a great relationship with them. Their two daughters and son participated in events from foreign missions to hiking trips. The family supported our youth ministry on every other front. But they felt disappointed in this one area.

This mother and father continued to stand by their convictions, and I respected that. Yet they never demeaned me or pinned me to the wall while expressing their dissatisfaction. When other parents did not seem to agree, this mom and dad would allow the issue to die—until the next meeting, at least!

I hope this example of a positive, godly way to deal with limited disappointment helps you. And I pray that the following example will encourage you to avoid some of the pitfalls of expressing limited disappointment in nonconstructive ways.

During my second year at one church, I spent quite a bit of time planning a mystery weekend for the students. I lined up two days downtown for mostly service-oriented activities. The students and leaders would feed and hang out with homeless families as well as help in other capacities.

One reason I made the weekend a secret was that I didn't think as many students would get excited about a service project as they might about a river-rafting retreat. I wanted to snag some of the young people who never would have signed up for a service trip and help them see that working for the Lord cannot only be fulfilling but genuinely fun.

When I created a flier to promote the retreat, I hyped the mystery part but included a note at the bottom for parents: *Please contact me if you would like further information.* Then I provided my phone number at the church.

No sooner had I begun to get excited about the number of students who were signing up for this event than I got a call from the mom of one of the most involved students in our ministry. The mother was irate and accused me of undercutting parents' authority and setting myself above them by withholding information.

Trying to explain to this mom that I had no intention of keeping parents in the dark did not seem to calm her fury. I struggled with this conversation because I'd never had any interaction with this woman before her angry phone call. I didn't want to offend her further, but I *did* want to set the record straight.

This mother expressed her discontent with rage. I not only felt scolded like a child, but I felt genuinely frustrated. I did not feel motivated to make changes or listen to her diatribe. Instead, I found myself enduring her comments and then trying to get over them after I hung up the phone.

Speaking the truth in love and waiting to calm down before you express disappointment are not only biblical principles of communication, they also produce better results. I for one always feel more open to changing a situation that parents find temporarily frustrating if they articulate their concerns with respect and patience.

Remember, you will most likely experience some level of limited disappointment when your child participates in a youth ministry. Try to take some time to reflect before deciding whether to communicate your concerns. If you do need to convey your feelings, go directly to the offending party and speak words laced with love.

EXPANDED DISAPPOINTMENT

If you feel disappointed with the greater vision of a youth ministry, or the execution of a proposed vision, I'd call your feelings *expanded disappointment.*

Beyond a single event or a specific occurrence, expanded disappointment has to do with the patterns or modes of operation you've observed in a youth ministry.

When I began ministry at EFCC, the mother and father of a physically challenged young man approached me and asked what my action plan for special-needs students looked like. I confessed to them that I didn't have one.

Not only did they feel disappointed by this, they made it known.

Thankfully, they didn't do so in an ugly way, but I could tell they felt more than limited disappointment. In the midst of starting a brand-new ministry, I simply hadn't begun developing a strategy for meeting the special needs of challenged students. In fact, at the time, their son was my only special-needs student. Though I didn't want this mom and dad to feel discontented or unimportant, I couldn't live up to their expectations immediately. But another pastor and I have dialogued since then and plan to develop a strategy for ministering to special-needs students both now and into the future.

The steps for dealing with expanded disappointment will be quite similar to those I discussed for handling limited disappointment, with a few exceptions. Allow me to highlight these while quickly reviewing the steps I mentioned in the previous section.

First, you will still benefit from assessing the level of your disappointment and determining whether and to whom you should express your displeasure.

When dealing with expanded disappointment, however, I'd recommend asking yourself two more questions:

1. Is this a matter of preference or personality difference?
2. Am I majoring in the minors?

Sometimes people feel generally disappointed with a ministry because the youth pastor or leader's style does not match their own. Unfortunately, there's not much one can do about this type of dissatisfaction, aside from finding a ministry that better suits your personality.

On the other hand, if you discover that you are majoring in the minors, I'd encourage you to revisit the chapter on healthy expectations.

One of Webster's definitions of *disappointment* is "free from illusion." Isn't that interesting? We often feel disenchanted with something because we have illusions of what it can or should be. When a ministry doesn't live up to our expectations, we feel let down and frustrated. But it may be *our* attitude that needs adjusting rather than someone else's.

Another great definition of *disappointment*—"the restless aspiration for improvement"—gives us a clue about how to deal with expanded disappointment. While you should strive for excellence and look for ways to improve things, a restless aspiration will exhaust both you and those with whom you're discontented. *Keep insatiable longings for change in check* while serving alongside youth pastors and leaders to help them and their ministries grow.

Here's something I tell students and encourage parents to think about as well: It's always easier to criticize from the bleachers. If you join the team and jump in as part of the solution, you're less likely to feel expanded disappointment.

In my experience, most expanded disappointment occurs when change takes place. A new youth pastor or leader may face the widespread disappointment of his flock of students and parents simply because he doesn't do things the good old way.

Long-beloved leaders who try something new or want to shake things up a bit may also face widespread discontent. Therefore, I'd ask you parents to add this step to your strategy for dealing with dissatisfaction: *Wait until you're sure a true pattern has developed.* What you believe may be a pattern, or a failure, might not turn out to be so in a few months.

Give any change (or any plan with which you're unhappy) some time, and see if a turnaround in the situation—or in your heart—occurs. Proverbs 21:23 says, "Whoever guards his mouth and tongue keeps his soul from troubles" (NKJV). Holding your tongue for a season may protect you from difficulty later.

Ecclesiastes 7:8 also points out that "the end of a thing is better than its beginning; the patient in spirit is better than the proud in spirit" (NKJV). Something may start out shaky but grow into a great ministry eventually. Don't assume you know the outcome (which reveals a prideful heart), but instead exercise a patient spirit.

I'd add one final guideline for dealing with disappointment: *Expect and commit to be in it for the long haul.* You will not see changes in goals or values immediately. Such things cannot be altered overnight. If you feel strongly enough about your disappointment, you will stay faithful to the cause, always seeking to speak truth in love.

If the conflict or your discontentment does not dissipate over time, you *can* find another youth ministry for your child. There's nothing wrong with disagreements within the body of Christ; it all depends on whether the parties involved can reach agreement or choose to go their separate ways.

OVERALL DISAPPOINTMENT

Over the course of my fourteen years in youth ministry, I've encountered much limited and expanded disappointment. I've also seen my share of overall disappointment.

This type of dissatisfaction encompasses not only youth ministry but also the larger church. Overall disappointment, usually quite complex, includes comprehensive discontent with the methods and/or goals of the greater church. Because of its wide-reaching nature, overcoming overall disappointment may necessitate the cooperation of the church's lay leaders, pastoral staff, and elders.

I'll give you an example that may help flesh out the type of disappointment I'm describing.

Scott started to feel disappointed sometime after he and his family began worshiping at their local church. They wanted to stay connected, so Scott prayed that God would give him insight into the real problems the church was experiencing as well as wisdom for how to communicate with the leaders about these issues.

Since part of his frustration centered on his son's growth in the youth ministry, Scott determined to start a small group in his home. With great success he developed a Bible study/fellowship group for his son and his son's closest friends. But the feelings of disappointment continued to gnaw at him.

Scott finally invited the senior pastor, Randy, out to lunch. He spent quite a bit of time praying before their meeting. Over lunch Scott shared with Randy some of the observations he felt led to articulate.

Whenever Scott talked about something pleasant, Randy responded and stayed fully engaged in the conversation. But if Scott made a comment that was somewhat challenging, Randy got a sort of glazed expression and stayed quiet.

Scott respected Randy's abilities as a pastor. He'd never known anyone better at visitation and hospitality. But his teaching, while accurate, always seemed to lack depth. Furthermore, Randy had little relationship with or authority over his staff.

Scott tried to articulate that the church seemed to suffer from a lack of vision. Proverbs 29:18 asserts, "Where there is no vision, the people perish" (KJV). He'd seen too many people stop attending worship services, in part because they felt a withering effect from being at a church with no purpose. Many parents either just dropped their kids off for youth-ministry events or led their entire family to another church. But discussing these things didn't even seem to get through to Randy.

Scott decided to set up a meeting with the head of the elder board. In talking with the elders, who ultimately assumed the responsibility for guiding the church, Scott hoped to convey his deep reservations about the course on which the congregation was set.

Before the appointment, Scott drafted a letter and sent it to Barry, the head elder. Scott outlined the topics he wanted to discuss in order to give Barry some time to think and pray. The meeting went amazingly well. Barry told Scott how encouraged he felt and expressed that it seemed as though Scott had been "reading his heart." Scott felt hopeful. But shortly after their lunch, Barry stepped down from the elder board and left the church.

When a new youth pastor came on board, Scott developed a great relationship with him. He discussed his issues with Kevin at length and was excited about Kevin's vision for youth ministry. But that vision never caught hold at the top.

Scott's wife, Brittany, finally approached him, indicating that she wanted them to look for a different church. He and Brittany did begin worshiping with another congregation but planned to stay active as leaders in the youth ministry of their previous church so that their son and daughter could continue to participate.

The remaining elders felt, however, that if Scott didn't attend the church, he could not stay on the youth-ministry staff. Kevin ultimately agreed, though he grieved the loss of a friend and leader.

The consequences of these circumstances reverberated through the entire church and into the youth ministry, sending ripples of discontentment and even destruction that lasted for many years.

If you, like Scott, sense overall disappointment with a church—disappointment that affects but does not center around the youth ministry—I encourage you to follow the strategies for facing limited and expanded disappointment that I outlined earlier.

Beyond putting those things into practice, however, I ask you to consider doing some of the things Scott did.

- *Spend time in prayer,* asking God to direct your words and purify your motives.
- *Set up a meeting* (or a couple of meetings) with the senior pastor. You may want to meet with the head of the elder board as well.
- *Spend still more time in prayer,* listening to God's heart on the matter.
- *Send a letter to the pastor (or elder) before your meeting* to prepare him for your comments and allow him time, as you have had, to process your concerns and pray. Pepper your letter with love and validation. (For help with this, see the next chapter, "How to Constructively Criticize a Ministry.")

- *Wait to see if change takes place.* While you watch and wait, try to be as big a part of the solution as you can be.
- If you see no resolution within a reasonable amount of time and continue to experience overall disappointment, *ask God to clearly show you whether He's leading your family to another church.* The decision to leave a church should not be made lightly, but if you've addressed your concerns biblically and are unable to resolve the issues over time, this may be your only reasonable course of action.

WHEN YOUR CHILD FEELS DISAPPOINTED

You may not feel limited, expanded, or overall disappointment with the church or youth ministry, but what if your son or daughter expresses discontentment?

Taking time to help them process their frustrations (*genuinely listening without judgment* to their concerns), evaluating the importance of the issues, and approaching whoever may be in charge of the areas or methods with which your child feels frustrated certainly works in these situations as well.

Speaking the truth in love and helping your child learn to do so—as well as refraining from gossiping with others about your child's concerns (or your own)—remains essential. But I'd also counsel you to think about some additional factors.

First, ask yourself, "Do I see this problem only through my child's eyes?" What works for others may be frustrating for your child. What works for your son or daughter may be unprofitable for others. *Try to keep in balance what a youth ministry can do for each individual. Attempt, when possible, to get beyond your son's or daughter's perspective* by discussing the issues with the youth pastor or leaders.

Another factor to keep in mind is that your child may feel disappointed because things have changed. Two instances when this occurred in my life are worth relating here.

After first arriving at a new church, I sensed that I did things differently than the previous youth pastor. It didn't bother me much until I took a team down to the inner city for an overnight service retreat.

Some of the students grumbled about being "forced to do a quiet time." They resisted going to sleep—"We never had a lights-out time when Don was around." They complained and they griped, and I ultimately decided to keep them at the church where we were staying, while the rest of the team traveled to a nearby park to cook for and serve the needy.

I got the complaining students into a circle and asked what was going on. These were the core students of the former youth group. They'd been at the church for a long time and were the power players.

They told me how they felt disappointed with some of the changes I'd made. They also said that the structured quiet time (they'd always chosen when and how to do their devotions) and being told when to go to bed were issues, though minor ones.

Later some of these same students thanked me for helping establish a structure that aided them in the disciplines of Bible study and service.

The second instance took place when I came on board at EFCC and changed the youth-group structure from large-group meetings to small-group fellowship/Bible study meetings. I faced quite a bit of opposition at first, specifically from those who wanted to be with friends (mostly of the opposite sex) who weren't in their core group.

One guy talked to me at a football game and expressed his displeasure with the new structure. He told me that he and his girlfriend always talked about what they learned at church, and now they couldn't do that because they'd been separated. I tried to believe that his motivation in telling me this was pure, but I remained suspicious of the reason he gave for his disappointment in the change.

At one point, this student's parents came to a meeting during which I communicated my reasons for switching to core groups as well as my vision for facilitating personal discipleship for each student through these small groups. These parents caught up to me afterward and thanked me, expressing how glad they were that they had come to the meeting, since all they'd heard about core groups from their son was negative. They wanted him to be involved after hearing my vision and purpose.

A third factor I'd encourage you to think about when addressing your child's discontentment is that students are sometimes disappointed with a youth ministry because they don't like new boundaries that leaders have set. I used to receive weekly communications (including name, address, and phone number to make sure I knew who wrote them) from a young man who wrote comments like "Jeramy's a lame drummer."

I tried to get to know this student, but every Sunday I had to ask him to stay in church rather than ditch. I finally called his dad and told him what had been happening week to week. After hearing my perspective, this father decided to require that his son join him in "big church" each Sunday.

All this to say, don't assume that what you hear from your child is 100 percent accurate. Certainly take the time to listen to his or her feelings, but take equal time to hear from the offending party before you cast judgment.

If your child expresses appropriate disappointment and you've met with the youth pastor or leaders with little or no result, you might consider starting a youth ministry in your home. You'd do this prayerfully, with the youth pastor's blessing. And you'd need to do it under his authority to avoid competing with the student ministry at the church—such as scheduling meetings for the same night so that students have to choose between groups, presenting your group to students as the better option, and so on.

Try to help your child see that there is great value in staying loyal and connected both to a youth ministry and to the greater church body. If you can, encourage your child to attend those events or services that he or she doesn't find disappointing.

Remember, your son or daughter will often mirror the ways you deal with discontentment. You can help your child grow into a mature Christian by modeling Christlike ways of facing dissatisfaction.

FALLING THROUGH THE CRACKS

A final note to moms and dads who sense that their child might be falling through the cracks of a youth ministry. It can be frustrating for any parent whose child just doesn't seem well connected with a group. The cause may simply be limited disappointment. It may be expanded or overall disappointment. Or it may be a personal problem unrelated to the youth ministry.

Whatever seems to be the reason for your child's disconnectedness, try to employ the strategies mentioned throughout this chapter. But if these strategies don't work, here are some other ways you can keep your child from slipping through the cracks of a ministry:

1. *Encourage your child to get to know other Christians at school and at church.* Your son or daughter may feel better connected if he or she invites friends to church or begins to make new friends at youth group. Some students merely need a bit of prodding to get to know others.

2. *Go with your son or daughter to an event and watch how he or she interacts with peers.* This may help you understand some of the reasons behind the discontentment. Your presence may also help your child feel safe at youth group, especially if he or she is younger.

3. *Ask your child to pick one youth-ministry activity a month that sounds appealing.* Offer to pay for your child and one friend to attend. That way your son or daughter will have someone to

sit with and have fun with. Fond memories of these events may help your child build a connection with the youth ministry.

4. *Ask a youth leader or volunteer to meet one-on-one with your child.* It's amazing how having just one person recognize and seek him or her out helps a young person feel important and wanted in a student ministry. Perhaps you can enlist a leader to help your child overcome feelings of disappointment (see Sue's story at the end of this chapter).

5. *"Talk it up."* Speak highly of the youth ministry. Try not to say things like "so-and-so's daughter *really* loves youth group," but instead focus on general comments such as "I see the student ministry is going to Mexico; that sounds like a lot of fun. What do you think?"

6. *Forcing participation may not be your best option.* Forcefully demanding participation in youth events is a far cry from gently prodding your child. I find that students who are forced to attend youth events usually sit in the back with their arms folded, totally closed to what anyone has to say. Ask yourself if another place might be a better fit for your son or daughter for a season. Maybe he or she would flourish by serving in another capacity, or maybe he or she would be grateful for youth group after sitting with you in your Sunday-school class! (Not that your class is bad. It's just not a student's territory.)

7. *Find out what's really going on.* Your son or daughter may have had a bad experience with some friends or with a person of the opposite sex in youth group. Something more serious may be going on. Try to dig down to the root of what's causing the disconnectedness.

My genuine desire, and I think I speak for most youth workers here, is that *no* student would fall through the cracks. Help us and allow us to help you as we are able. Let's partner together to keep students connected with and thriving in youth ministry.

After you read the next chapter, I'd encourage you to revisit this chapter. You can't deal with disappointment in a healthy or godly manner without cultivating the skill of constructive criticism. I earnestly hope that these two chapters might equip you to honor the Lord as you face the challenges that come not only in youth ministry but also in life.

What Parents Like You Had to Say

From Sue, a youth worker:

When I first started working with a small group of girls, I thought it would be easy to make friends with them. They were juniors, after all, not squirrelly freshmen. But instead of welcoming me with open arms, the girls acted cool. That is, until their parents invited me to attend a track meet in which two of them ran. The girls saw me standing on the sidelines cheering, and somehow it broke through that I *really* cared, not just about their spiritual growth, but also about them as people. Afterward, one of the girls sprinted to me and gave me a hug. Meeting the students on their turf went a long way in helping me connect with them. It would have been easy to give up in disappointment, but somehow, through watching "my girls" run, God enabled me to see that frustration does not have to lead to abandonment. I'm grateful that these parents partnered with me to overcome their daughters' disconnectedness.

From Graham, father of three, all college students now. (*Author's note:* When I interviewed Graham, I laughed because he could have written this chapter as well as, if not better, than I have. He just shot these things off the top of his head.)

Here's what I have found effective: Be direct. Don't gossip. Don't assume. Remember the anger of a man does not achieve the righteousness of God—and that whole passage in James 1. [Graham is referring here to James 1:20 and following.] And

I have needed to follow my own advice on several occasions. I think parents who take their roles seriously want to know who and what influences their child's spiritual growth. Too many things happen—even in a youth ministry—that can negatively impact a student. For instance, when my son got into some trouble at a youth event, I called the two youth leaders who were with him at the time. I had spoken with my son already and wanted to hear the perspective of the interns who had watched him make a pretty poor choice. Though I felt disappointed that they hadn't encouraged my son to make a better decision, I didn't go in with guns blazing. Instead, I tried to use the moment to teach and train these young men. They will most likely be fathers one day and will need to teach their own children the ways of the Lord, including how to deal with discontentment. I wanted to seize the chance to help them grow.

Eight

How to Constructively Criticize a Youth Ministry

When Peter asked if I could do breakfast with him, I looked forward to our appointment. Peter and I always had a great time breaking bread together (sourdough toast, to be specific), and our relationship had both depth and authenticity.

We met early on Friday, devoured Denver omelets, and drank far more coffee than was good for any human. After our meal and some catch-up conversation about family and ministry, Peter asked, "Can I share with you some of my feelings about where the youth group is headed?"

"Sure," I replied.

He reached down and brought out a legal pad. Notes scribbled from top to bottom covered the first sheet, and he flipped to check a second before he began.

I wondered what Peter would say first. I prepared myself for the worst, kind of like a football player does when he's on the line about to be hit.

Though I knew Peter well and felt his support for me, I couldn't help thinking this would be a tough conversation. So many times over my years in youth ministry, meetings like this have left me winded, sometimes even aching.

As Peter began, I listened intently. I allowed him to present several of his concerns, all of which I realized simply needed clarification to set aright. He'd heard "things" (a.k.a. church gossip), and I just had to give him the full story to set his mind at ease.

Peter then went on to recount to me something that had occurred on a Sunday two weeks earlier. I had been out of town with my wife and had left one of my interns, Wayne, in charge of Sunday school. He spoke that morning and shared with the students some of his past struggles.

While an essential aspect of youth ministry is comforting students with the comfort we as leaders have received (see 2 Corinthians 1)—whether in overcoming sin or going through trials beyond our control—the way in which my intern related his experimentation with certain sins was definitely inappropriate.

There's a saying that floats around youth-worker circles: What leaders do in moderation, students will do in excess. In Christ, pastors and leaders never have to be ashamed of the past. Yet we all need to exercise discernment in when and how we share so that students won't feel justified in sinning because leaders they respect did it when they were younger. As Peter pointed out, I needed to help Wayne learn this; I needed to correct him.

I sincerely thanked Peter for bringing this problem straight to me. I want to be the first one to hear about anything that happens that might negatively impact the youth ministry. All too frequently people "share" among themselves, conversations swirl, and before you know it, misinformation and half-truths breed anxiety and dissension.

As a pastor I've been given responsibility over a ministry by God. He's asked me to be both protector and guard, like a shepherd who looks out for the safety and health of his sheep. I feel honored when a parent helps me in this immense task and comes to me right away with a concern.

Another thing Peter communicated that morning was that he felt a comment I'd made the Sunday after our local high-school prom could have been misconstrued. Many youth ministries have a tradition that after school dances guys and girls wear their suits and fancy dresses to church the next day. I told the young women that Sunday that they looked particularly beautiful.

Peter didn't want the girls to think that their outward appearance counted more than their hearts. His wife had struggled with an eating disorder and had worked for many years to balance the pursuit of inward beauty with outward care for her body.

While I understood his point, I did not agree with his criticism. Through the entire year our ministry highlighted the heart growth of our ladies. We made a concerted effort to encourage them to build a godly character rather than concentrating on their physical appearance. I simply felt the girls would benefit from a compliment, since a great deal of what they hear and think about themselves is negative.

I assured Peter that I shared his concern for the greater issue and that I would be aware of how any comment I made from up front might be received.

We talked for quite a while (as you might imagine with two pages of notes!), and I felt genuinely exhorted and encouraged by our conversation. I appreciate that Peter didn't simply yank his daughter out of the ministry or assume the worst about the group. Instead, he offered constructive criticism and ideas for how to approach some of the problems he'd observed.

I left with confidence and the recognition that I needed to attend to several things.

CONSTRUCTIVE—THE KEYWORD

Nothing makes most of us tense up (or as your child might say, "freak out") more readily than an undeserved, unsolicited, and tactless critique of our character, decisions, or work.

Yet as early twentieth-century author Elbert Hubbard noted, criticism is inescapable. "To avoid criticism," he declared, "do nothing, say nothing, be nothing." Whenever you act or speak, *someone* will disagree with your choices and methods.

So how can Christians criticize while still obeying Christ's command to encourage and build one another up (1 Thessalonians 5:11)? I believe we can do this by learning to *constructively* criticize.

What Peter offered me that morning at breakfast was *constructive criticism.* Some may think of this phrase as an oxymoron, but I've had the privilege of receiving some surprisingly uplifting critiques of my ministry.

Constructive criticism is more of what prominent businessman Jaime Walters calls an "information-sharing dialogue" than an opportunity for one person to vent while the other sits silently. During constructive criticism, both parties relate their perspectives and discuss possible misunderstandings as well as solutions for genuine problems.

I'll be honest: Criticizing constructively is *not* easy. It doesn't come naturally, and there's a real tension between the art of constructively criticizing and turning a conversation into the Spanish Inquisition. But developing skill in this area will help you not only interact with your youth leaders but with everyone else you know as well.

A note before we head into some practical suggestions: Determining the best way to constructively criticize in a given situation will depend largely on the personality and relationship dynamics involved. This chapter will provide some pointers to help you criticize constructively, but it doesn't offer exhaustive coverage of this subject's intricate nuances. Some highly instructive books have been written on constructive criticism, should you like more information.[1]

Criticizing Well

Before writing this chapter, I thought I'd see what *Webster's Dictionary* had to say about "criticism." I think looking at the definition of this word will help set the stage for the rest of this chapter.

The dictionary defines *criticism* as "the art of evaluating or analyzing with knowledge and propriety." Isn't that great? If you ask me, people who offered criticism according to this definition would *always* criticize constructively.

In order to critique helpfully, one must think about ("evaluate" and "analyze") what one would like to criticize. This indicates that criticism does not merely spring from feelings or rumors, but from a sincere consideration of what is happening.

One must also criticize with "knowledge and propriety." This means that you should get all the information you can (from the original source) about any situation before you critique. And you should do all of this with propriety; in other words, with decorum and respect.

Furthermore, the verb *criticize* means "to consider the merits and demerits of, and judge accordingly." Again, this would indicate to me that when we critique something, we should always weigh both the positive and negative sides of a given situation. In order to criticize well, we need to look at what is right, not just at what is wrong. We should form an opinion with awareness of *both* the good and the bad aspects of a situation.

Apart from simply looking at the definitions of these words, let me offer some suggestions for how to constructively criticize your youth leader or his ministry.

1. Constructive criticism works best in the context of a relationship. When two people share mutual respect and a common understanding, it's far easier for one or the other to offer words of critique. As I mentioned earlier, Peter and I had several positive interactions before he came to me with his concerns.

Too often parents contact me only when they want to criticize the ministry. While I know it's not always possible for a parent to develop a relationship with me (or one of my leaders) before he or she expresses a concern, it definitely improves an information-sharing dialogue if I know a little bit about his or her personality and preferences. In addition, if I have a relationship with a parent who I already *know* wants to partner with and build up the ministry, I can receive his or her criticism with greater confidence. As Proverbs 27:9 says, "The heartfelt counsel of a friend is as sweet as perfume and incense" (NLT). When offered by a friend, constructive criticism can be the type of heartfelt counsel this verse describes.

I call this kind of criticism "organic" because it comes out of a shared bond of trust and respect. As you interact with others, including friends, you'll disagree with some of what they do or say. Yet within an established relationship, people are better able to instinctively offer and receive constructive criticism.

2. Constructive criticism helps us avoid the rumor mill. God commands us not to "bear false witness against" against others (Exodus 20:16, KJV) or to "lie about them" (Proverbs 24:28, NLT). Believers bear the weighty responsibility of revealing to a slander-hungry world that we "speak the truth in love" (Ephesians 4:15). It grieves me when I see Christians participate in hurtful rumormongering, and it wounds me and other pastors when the slander is directed at us.

Proverbs 26:22 states, "What dainty morsels rumors are—but they sink deep into one's heart" (NLT). It's certainly easy to join in conversations that tear someone apart. Sometimes it's even deliciously fun as this proverb points out. Yet that scripture also bluntly discloses the results of dining on the "dainty morsels" of slander: Words sink deep into the heart. They are like arrows that lodge in the most tender and vulnerable places in us and those around us.

Whenever you have a grievance or a concern, you can decide whether you will go directly to the person responsible or engage in maligning someone's character. Make an active choice to avoid the rumor mill.

Beware of using spiritual language—such as, "Would you pray with me about this?" or "Can I share with you something that is really burdening my heart?"—to mask slanderous comments. As a believer you will know when you're speaking out of a true desire for counsel or a destructive yearning for scandal.

Proverbs 16:28 reveals that "a troublemaker plants seeds of strife; gossip separates the best of friends" (NLT). Not only will you alienate the person of whom you speak poorly, but you also run the risk of pushing your closest friends away with your wagging tongue.

Again, I encourage you to extinguish the fires of gossip. Proverbs 26:20 brings a great truth to light: "Fire goes out for lack of fuel, and quarrels disappear when gossip stops" (NLT). Avoiding the rumor mill will prevent your criticisms from turning into a raging fire of conflict.

As a final note, be careful what and how you share with your child. An undiscerning remark may cause your son or daughter to distrust or even dislike the youth pastor and leaders. Unless you encourage your child to trust and respect spiritual leaders, his or her spiritual growth may be compromised.

3. Examine your heart. Before you approach a youth pastor or leader with a criticism, ask the Lord to help you separate your emotions from the offense (what actually happened or is happening). Every situation involves facts and feelings, so before you try to critique constructively, I recommend finding a balance between the two. If you criticize based on emotions alone, you may undermine your ideas or concerns. On the other hand, coldly rehearsing facts may wound someone unnecessarily.

Also, ask God to help you criticize actions and behaviors, not people. Unless a serious character issue is involved, focus your words on what has been done or decided, not on what you see as a leader's failures. This fundamental rule of communication makes information-sharing dialogues more constructive than destructive.

In addition, ask God to reveal whether you can offer your comments authentically and honestly. Criticism is more constructive when the person who offers it comes to the table without hypocrisy. The well-known verse from Matthew 7:3 certainly applies here: "Why do you look at the speck of sawdust in your brother's eye and pay no attention to the plank in your own eye?" Someone with a log in his or her eye cannot see clearly and therefore cannot help another person work on character issues or decision making.

Job 36:13 tells us that "the hypocrites in heart heap up wrath" (KJV). Sometimes people criticize because their own inauthenticity leads to anger, which they unleash on others.

Examine your heart before you decide to criticize. With a pure heart and a clear conscience, you'll be better able to critique helpfully.

4. Review your assumptions and expectations. Murky or unvoiced assumptions and expectations make it nearly impossible to offer constructive feedback. Not only do they create problems in communicating your thoughts, they also prevent you from accurately assessing a given situation.

Before you criticize, bounce your proposed criticism off a spouse or trusted friend (who won't tempt you to gossip!). Most of us automatically assume that what we know or feel is right. If this is true, it follows that everyone else is wrong. Take some time to evaluate whether you've presumed too much. With the counsel of others, you'll find it easier to approach a youth pastor or leader with as few false assumptions as possible.

Even after talking with someone, you may still harbor incorrect assumptions. When you meet with a youth pastor or leader, ask questions to establish whether your assumptions are correct. This will help the two of you remain on the same page as you dialogue and share information.

It's also beneficial to determine whether the pastor or leader thinks your expectations are realistic. Genuinely try to understand how the youth worker views his or her role. Use disarming statements, such as "I thought I understood _____" or "I believe you prioritize _____." Placing the weight of assumption on yourself can help the two of you avoid an offensive-defensive conversation.

Also remember that others can flourish in circumstances you find intolerable. Your criticism may involve matters of preference, style, or your personal sense of justice. When offering feedback in these situations, you might begin with an unthreatening statement, such as "Like you, I want to see the ministry thrive. I'd love to share with you a thought about _____."

You may want to review the chapter on expectations (chapter 1) before you offer suggestions to a pastor or leader. If you're expecting perfection from a youth worker, you'll never be satisfied. Like you, pastors and leaders will make the wrong decisions from time to time. They, too, mess up! Sometimes it falls on leaders to try to correct situations that are out of their control. Help them overcome any poor choices and/or unforeseeable difficulties rather than making them feel worse. And remember Paul's words in Colossians 3:13: "Bear with each other and forgive whatever grievances you may have against one another. Forgive as the Lord forgave you." When your criticism involves a leader's sin or misjudgments, extend Christ's grace and forgiveness.

Finally, check to see if you're expecting someone else to fix a problem at home that needs your attention. Sometimes hurting parents try to blame the church for the troubles their child is facing. Just make sure you're not criticizing the youth staff for something that really requires your own intervention.

5. Review your intentions. This final review flows naturally out of a review of your heart and your assumptions and expectations. If your heart is pure and you've aligned your assumptions and hopes with realistic and accurate information, your intentions will most likely be appropriate. Yet there are times when even Christians exploit a situation to get a pound of flesh.

This happened to me the first summer after I began a new ministry. The elders and pastors agreed to let Jerusha and me take a week of vacation after our two-week mission trip overseas. Two other adult leaders would chaperon the team of students home.

One father had a difficult time when he heard about this plan. He wanted to offer his thoughts on the situation, but instead of making constructive suggestions, he came to me in total frustration: "I don't think it's right for you to use the mission trip to get a vacation. I don't get to take a week off after my business trips even though I'd like to see some of the places I have to go. It's absolutely not appropriate."

Though I had the full support of every other set of parents on the team, this one man could not accept the elder board's blessing and the consensus of his peers. Even though I heard him out and apologized for any misunderstandings to which I may have contributed, this father insisted on meeting with me and the head elder. That meeting ended with the elder saying, "Roger, Jeramy has already explained himself three times. You just want a pound of his flesh, and I won't allow it."

Though I left the meeting without a resolution of the problem, Roger approached me in the airport just before the team departed and apologized.

If you simply want to tear into somebody because you're unhappy with what's going on, you feel something's unfair, or you want to make sure someone knows what he or she has done wrong, be careful! Ask the Lord to purify your intentions and help you set a godly agenda.

Finally, remember that "your own soul is nourished when you are kind, but you destroy yourself when you are cruel" (Proverbs 11:17, NLT). When you offer constructive criticism with good intentions, no one will be destroyed.

6. Cool off before you criticize. It's unlikely you'll be able to offer helpful criticism unless you get a handle on your emotions before you speak to another person. While you may be frustrated or even extremely angry, heated feelings rarely facilitate a healthy information-sharing dialogue. Try not to offer feedback in a state of panic or volatility.

As Proverbs 15:18 reminds us, "A hot-tempered man [or woman!] stirs up dissension, but a patient man calms a quarrel." Anger or irritation usually leads to conflict rather than constructive criticism.

An oft-quoted verse in Ephesians commands Christians to "be angry, and do not sin" (4:26, NKJV). Ask God to dissipate any fury so that you can share your concerns with grace.

In addition, avoid confrontation when you're anxious about the meeting or feeling resentful. These heightened emotions can also lead to poor communication.

Finally, place the discussion in proper perspective. Simply put, some things are more important than others. Attempt to determine whether you're allowing circumstances to become a bigger deal to you than they need to be.

7. Prepare your thoughts before you offer feedback. I encourage you to sort out your thoughts on an issue before you approach someone with a criticism. Write them out, even practice what you want to say, if necessary. This will make your information-sharing dialogue run more smoothly and help you to accurately present your ideas.

8. Time your criticism for success. One Wednesday night, about five minutes before we'd scheduled our youth group's departure for an event, a mother approached me and launched into a critique of our system for organizing medical-release forms.

The concerns she expressed were valid and her ideas were good, but I simply couldn't dialogue with her because it wasn't the right time. Had she made an appointment with me, I could have really listened and asked for her help in establishing a more efficient method. Instead, I felt pulled in several directions and unable to respond appropriately to her suggestions.

Right before Sunday school, Bible study, or really *any* event, youth pastors and leaders usually feel frantic enough without being asked to field concerns or criticism. They're often juggling lots of details and needs. Most likely, not only will leaders feel unable to meet your needs at those times, but such untimely criticism may discourage them just when they're trying to minister to students.

Though before or after an event may be the only time you run into the youth pastor or leader, exercise restraint and use discernment. I think the

King James translation of Ecclesiastes 3:7 says it well: There is "a time to keep silence, and a time to speak." Learning when to "keep silence" and when to speak will help you in all conversations, not just ones involving criticism.

9. *Whenever possible, speak to a person face to face.* In many ways this point explains itself. If you must call or write (like the concerned parents in chapter 7), remember that the youth pastor or leader will not be able to read your facial expression or body language. This may confuse your communication.

I know it's not always possible to catch a leader face to face. Your schedules may perpetually conflict. I simply encourage you to criticize in person if possible.

As a side note: If you're married, it's best if your spouse accompanies you when you meet with a pastor or leader. While one person may misunderstand a comment, two people can help each other sort through their perceptions about a conversation. Furthermore, you'll save yourself the effort of communicating to your spouse what happened when you offered your feedback.

10. *Place criticism between encouragements.* I read once that whenever you have criticism to offer, you should "sandwich" it between statements that build up and validate the other person.

Try to make a list of four positive qualities of the staff person and the ministry in general. This will help you begin and end your conversation with some uplifting comments.

No one ever hears *too much* affirmation. In fact, studies show that most people feel harshly criticized more than encouraged at work. I want to share with you that in youth ministry "seldom is heard an encouraging word." Many youth pastors burn out quickly (sadly, the turnover rate for youth leaders is high) because of interpersonal problems or the weight of people's unmet, and often unhealthy, expectations.

If you cannot think of anything positive to say, ask the Lord to reveal

His love for the person or ministry. Should you remain unable to think of some supportive words, ask someone else what he or she most appreciates about the leader.

Proverbs 13:14 reminds us that "the advice of the wise is like a life-giving fountain" (NLT). I'm sure all of us want life to overflow from our lips the way this verse describes. We can try to fulfill this hope by wisely advising according to the "sandwich principle."

Finally, let me share with you a practical side to this point. Charles M. Schwab once remarked, "In my wide associations in life, meeting with many and great men in various parts of the world, I have yet to find the man, however great or exalted his station, who did not do better work and put forth greater effort under a spirit of approval than he would ever do under a spirit of criticism."

Not only will you give life to others through encouraging feedback, you may also spur the youth pastor or leader on to greater success than if you criticize without supporting him as well.

11. Try to remember that most youth pastors want to do what's right and good. Otherwise, they wouldn't have gotten into ministry! Most youth pastors and leaders would like to improve their approach and hone their skills in serving people. Sharing constructive criticism with them will help them achieve these goals.

Someone once communicated to me that our method of compiling student information might be improved. Though I knew it would be a huge undertaking, I truly appreciated her ideas and asked her to help me put them into practice.

Pastors and volunteers sometimes feel a sense of failure precisely because others seem to assume the worst about them. Leaders don't always know how to deal with particular situations, but you can be sure that most of the time they *want* to do what's best.

12. Keep criticism constructive by using the right manner, tone, and place for your criticism. It's probably obvious that your tone of voice and your nonverbal cues make a *huge* difference in the way a person receives your criticism. Attitudes come through loud and clear even if words have been carefully chosen.

Constructive criticism maintains respect and dignity for both parties from the beginning of a conversation and even after the discussion draws to a close. Yelling, scolding, or "talking at" someone demeans both people participating in a dialogue.

Once while I was running an event attended by close to six hundred students and fifty adult leaders, eighty significant decisions for Christ were made. As a small group of us began to pray and rejoice, a parent who had come to volunteer burst into the room and literally started yelling at me in front of my five staff members.

After I explained what we were doing, he said, "Well, that's good, but you can't be in here when things are out of control outside."

He went on to inform me that for some time students had been trying to leave the premises, and he didn't know how to make them stay. This was definitely something that needed my attention, but it was the first I had heard about the situation. Instead of coming and informing me, he assumed I didn't care because I hadn't shown up to help him and the other volunteers man the parking lot.

This parent had something important to tell me, but he did so in an inappropriate way. His tone and manner were aggressive. Moreover, he embarrassed me and my staff by making a public display of his criticism. Constructive criticism happens best in private and in a rational manner. That way feedback can be shared and understood.

Finally, remember that "a quarrelsome person starts fights as easily as hot embers light charcoal or fire lights wood" (Proverbs 26:21, NLT). Approach people in the right manner and place, and you'll most likely avoid igniting an unnecessary fight.

13. Choose nonthreatening words. I like the way the *New Living Translation* illuminates Ephesians 4:29: "Don't use foul or abusive language. Let everything you say be good and helpful, so that your words will be an encouragement to those who hear them."

In addition to using the right tone and manner in speech, you can choose to avoid using words that will only make another person defensive. Try to steer clear of judgmental statements or indictments. Also keep away from hot-button words that may alienate the other person. If you don't know what words might be "foul or abusive," "hot," or "judgmental," ask someone else. That may help you avoid potentially harmful comments.

Additionally, instead of "you" statements—"You never," "You don't," "You must," "You should," etc.—try to use "I" statements—"I feel," "I hope," "I would like," "I think." This can set the stage for a positive response rather than a defensive reaction.

14. Keep your comments short and to the point. It really helps to limit your criticism to one or two topics. Don't "scatter gun" a pastor or leader with so many issues that he can't process what you've said. Presenting a litany of concerns or, worse, the person's shortcomings will most likely overload the conversation.

15. Make sure you and the other person are on the same page. As I mentioned with regard to expectations, it's critical (so to speak) that you and the person you've approached with a criticism are on the same page. Ask questions to clarify that what you've heard is actually what the pastor or leader intended to say. See if the pastor or leader can accurately articulate what you've stated as well. The last thing you want is for an information-sharing dialogue to end poorly as the result of misperceptions.

16. Speak for yourself. Try not to include others in your criticism ("Some of us parents feel...," "Lots of people are saying...," etc.). Speak only for yourself and, if necessary, for your child or family.

Should others approach you to head up or join a "combined effort" aimed at criticizing a youth pastor or leader, graciously ask them to speak to the person themselves. Even if you, too, feel disappointed with the same situation, do not "gang up" on a youth worker. Instead, encourage others to approach a youth worker individually and present their suggestions and concerns clearly.

17. Invest your time and energy to find a solution. Henry Ford once declared, "Don't find the mistake, but the solution." Too often people lob a grenade of criticism and then run out of the way. I make this plea on behalf of many pastors and leaders: "Come and help, please!"

Solving problems is hard work. Yet real progress can be made if you take a team approach to criticism. Using statements like "Can I look at something with you?" or "Can we brainstorm about something?" establishes a mutual goal and places you and the pastor or leader on the same page. Show that you truly care about the youth ministry by being willing to help make change possible.

18. Remember that change takes time. Be as patient as possible. Criticism often brings about immediate solutions for urgent needs or issues, but it cannot change the course of a ministry overnight. The Lord encourages us to be long-suffering, as He is (see Galatians 5:22). Give the youth pastor or leader the benefit of the doubt, and stay put to see what God will do as a result of the conversation you had.

Sometimes change doesn't occur. The person you spoke with may respond defensively or reject your ideas. If so, think about the following two suggestions.

19. Purpose to remain dignified in the face of defensiveness. You always have the choice to reflect Christ no matter how a confrontation goes. Choose to respond with grace if a pastor or leader responds defensively to constructive criticism.

In addition, before you discount a pastor or leader because he has become disheartened or defensive after being criticized, keep the following in mind:

- Pastors, too, have rotten days. You may simply have caught someone at a bad time. Try again and pray for the best.

- A number of what-ifs may have hindered the conversation. Be as sensitive as you can to the many things that are going on in a pastor's life, family, and ministry. Always try to use a healthy dose of empathy!
- Could anything you said have been interpreted as attacking or unkind? Ask and, when necessary, apologize.
- Do you and this person have a history of bad communication? If so, things may have gone wrong from the get-go. Pursue reconciliation with the person and wait until you've gotten off to a new start before you once again present your critique.
- Did you offer your help or just vent your frustrations? If you think you may have lobbed a grenade of criticism, call back and see if you can invest in a solution.
- Think how you react when you're criticized. Not many people like to hear what's wrong with their work. Again, empathize as much as you can!

If after pondering these things you still feel that the pastor or leader behaved inappropriately, you may be dealing with a maturity problem or a character issue. I suggest that you try again to talk with the person, and if you do not get a better hearing, approach his or her supervisor to set up a meeting with the three of you.

20. Be willing to accept rejection. The youth pastor or leader may decide against implementing the changes you've suggested. His response may be due to a difference of opinion or it could reflect pride or an unwillingness to accept criticism.

Either way, prayerfully consider your response. Try not to make rash decisions that may hurt you, your child, or anyone else.

If you believe the person is sinning, you can approach him or her according to Matthew 18:15-18. (To review the principle Jesus sets forth: First, confront the person yourself. If he or she does not respond, go back with one or two mature Christians. If he or she still refuses to hear a rebuke, take the issue to the church.)

When the issue is one of style, preference, or expectation, however, you have several options: You can become more involved in the youth ministry in an attempt to effect change, you can withdraw your teen from the youth group and plug him or her into some other ministry at the church, or you can be led by God to another church altogether.

Acts 15 chronicles the separation of two godly apostles, Paul and Barnabas. They disagreed, they parted ways, and both went on to minister. If you do need to separate yourself from a situation, do it the way these men of God did—separate with grace and dignity, not with backbiting and gossip.

WRAP-UP

The conclusion of the matter is this: Constructive criticism takes time and practice, both to give and receive.

I like the way Jaime Walters puts it: "Being critical is easy, and offering criticism seems easier still. Yet constructive criticism—the more refined and effective brand of feedback—is like an art."[2]

No one becomes an artist without some effort. Work on your skills, and you will be able to approach not only leaders and pastors in a youth ministry but anyone you may wish to criticize constructively.

What Parents Like You Had to Say

From Kathy, mother of two boys, one in high school and one in junior high:

I think people have a hard time criticizing constructively for two reasons: First, they wait too long to address the situation. Generally, people like to avoid confrontation, so they often wait until anger motivates them to speak their mind. But when anger rather than compassionate concern becomes the motivating force behind a confrontation, it's almost impossible for someone to criticize constructively.

Second, many people do not really believe you can be genuinely disappointed in or angry about what someone does or says and yet still confront that person in love. Consequently, they either water down the issue, trying not to rock the boat, or they put a phony "God will take care of it" glaze over the problem. This can hinder constructive criticism as much as anger can.

I've found that the best way to confront a dissatisfying (and even sinful) situation is to approach it with humility and gentleness. If people know I care about what happens and, more important, that I care about them, they seem better able to handle any critique I may offer.

In doing this, however, I believe it's important to clearly and lovingly speak the *truth*. What's the point of bringing an issue to light if you don't get to the bottom of what has caused the discontent and frustration?

Finally, I work at offering my criticism as a suggestion,

giving the other person the final choice. While manipulating or guilt tripping someone into agreeing with me or doing what I want may achieve short-term results, the long-term risks of alienating or angering that person are too great. Constructive criticism does not issue an edict; it proposes one possible solution for a problem.

I see constructive criticism as loving accountability. In criticizing constructively, you're helping another Christian stay focused on what God has called him or her to do and be. When compelled by love and directed with humble kindness, criticism can actually build up and edify someone. And *that's* constructive!

Nine

Youth Ministry Outside the Box

ONE SINGLE METHOD of ministry cannot meet the needs of every family. If the youth group at your home church does not offer everything you want or need, you have many options other than simply "pulling the plug" and attending a different church.

Youth ministry does not have to be limited to the four walls of a particular church. A student can be fed well by participating in a couple of different groups, each one fulfilling distinct needs.

In this chapter I'd like to describe some excellent ministries that fall outside the box of traditional church youth groups. I pray that in learning about the various options, you will find hope for a student or family who doesn't totally connect with a specific youth ministry.

Before you start reading, remember one last thing. Some of these sections may or may not apply to your family. Feel free to skim the subheadings in this chapter first and then bounce around to the ones that most pique your interest.

HOMESCHOOLED STUDENTS

Some homeschool students and families feel different from the general population of a youth ministry. Undoubtedly, distinctions can exist, and it's unrealistic to assume that all homeschool students and families will feel exactly the same about youth group as students who have been educated in public or private schools.

If your homeschooled child feels like an outsider in a youth ministry, you can take several approaches to help him or her either feel more connected or find other places to get needs met. For information on finding other options for youth fellowship, look at the section in this chapter titled "Beyond the Church Walls." If you want to stay exclusively within the church, think through the following possibilities.

One option is to create homeschool programs that mirror on-campus events. For instance, your son or daughter may feel left out because "everyone else" will be participating in something like See You at the Pole. To solve this problem, consider getting your child together with other homeschool students to pray around another public flagpole (perhaps at a park, a library, etc.). Not only will your child have similar experiences as other students in prayer and in public witness, but because your child did what everyone else did, he or she will also be able to join with public- and private-school friends in any postevent activities.

You may also wish to open your home to other students. You can even try to help your son's or daughter's friends understand and appreciate homeschooling and its benefits. This may help your child feel special rather than simply "different."

Another option is allowing your child to meet with a Young Life or Youth for Christ group (I will describe these later in the chapter). Since these ministries meet after school and off-campus, a homeschooled student may easily join with other Christian students after school hours.

Finally, as I've mentioned a couple of times in other chapters, you could start a small group for like-minded students. Or you could join with a youth ministry for corporate worship and then break into your own discipleship group when it's time for Bible study.

I'm sure you're getting the idea. Bottom line: You don't have to throw up your hands and conclude that your child will never connect with other like-minded students. Find out what options are available in your area, discuss them with your son or daughter, and jump in.

SINGLE-PARENT AND BLENDED FAMILIES

Family dynamics have grown more and more complex over the fourteen years I've worked in youth ministry. The term *family* can mean many things to my students and their loved ones.

If your child comes from a unique family situation, it would be helpful if you let your youth pastor or leader know what to expect and how best to minister to your child. For instance, if your son or daughter spends every other weekend away from the local church, you may want to give the leadership a heads-up. That way someone won't be calling your child twice a month and asking, "Where were you on Sunday?" This kind of question may make a student feel embarrassed about his or her family situation.

Also, make the youth ministers aware of any name differences. This will help everyone avoid awkward communications.

If you sense the youth pastor or leader classifying or categorizing your family as "different," prayerfully consider talking with him or her. Single parenting, divorce, a death in the family, or guardianship by grandparents are not the defining characteristics of your family's identity.

Those in blended families may want to think about letting the youth pastor or leaders know about any stepsibling dynamics that could impact the ministry.

And if you have specific financial needs or strains, let the youth ministers know. Our church offers scholarships for parents who want their children to attend events but just can't make it work with their budget. God is the Great Provider; He uses youth ministries to help if those in need will simply ask. I know that parents may feel uncomfortable asking for help, but youth leaders are longing to serve and help them.

The family of God is your greater family, and I pray that you would feel a part of the youth ministry as much as your son or daughter does. It must thrill God's heart when youth leaders can act as father figures for the fatherless, offer maternal love to the motherless, and provide a place of comfort and acceptance for the lonely.

The church and the family need to work together to accomplish what God desires. We cannot labor independently; our work depends heavily on each other's support and cooperation.

I'd like to honor every family, and I pray that every family would grant me that same respect. Help me and other youth ministers honor you and assist you in the challenges of raising children.

Out-of-the-Area Students

When a new school year begins, one of our youth leaders often tries to pump students up by calling out the names of area schools and asking the students to scream in support of their alma maters. Sometimes we see which school can outscream the others.

Inevitably, we either forget a school that represents a smaller group of students or embarrass someone by calling the name of his or her school and listening to the ensuing silence. I *hate* situations like that. But I'm pretty sure the students I serve dislike it even more than I do.

When you attend a church that's a distance from your home, you run the risk that you or your child will feel "out of the community." This may not become clear until a student enters a youth ministry in which pastors or leaders are more likely to talk about local schools and their activities, or worse, when leaders plan events while an under-represented school is still in session.

Again, you do not need to find another church, although you may want to consider the benefits of worshiping with a body closer to home. If you do stay at your current church, you may never be able to avoid minor incidents like screaming-for-your-school situations. You do, however, have some great options for helping your child stay connected in the most important ways.

First, I recommend that you find other students at your child's school who attend the same church you do. Offer to carpool and try to build relationships between the families. It's especially helpful if you can do this when students are most open to making new friends, typically during their first couple years of involvement in youth ministry.

Second, think about how you talk to your son or daughter while driving to youth events. If your child feels that driving to a church event is a burden to you, he or she may be less excited about participating in a ministry. Moreover, your child may question the significance of church activities if it seems that fellowship with other believers is less of a priority than the other things in your schedule.

Third, make every effort to connect your child with the ministries available to him or her. If a midweek evening Bible study seems unfeasible because of a long drive, the family's need for dinner, your child's need to do homework, and your need to rest after a long day at work, you have a couple of options: You can either rearrange some activities on the day your son or daughter would like to go to church, or you can find another midweek ministry closer to your home. Even if your son or daughter doesn't go to this youth group regularly, he or she may find that attending another fellowship with a friend or serving at a local church (perhaps in a nursery or with an Awana program) can be extremely encouraging and faith building.

Beyond the Church Walls

Parachurch organizations, ministries that partner with churches in discipling young Christians, exist on or near many junior- and senior-high campuses. I'd like to describe a few for you, though this is by no means an exhaustive list. You can find out what's available at your son's or daughter's school by contacting other parents, national ministry headquarters (see the appendix for more information), or the school itself.

Clubs

Many schools allow and sometimes even sponsor faith-based clubs on their campuses. Students can worship and study the Bible together as well as share their faith with others in a way that is deemed acceptable by the school.

I wholeheartedly support Christian clubs on campus and recommend that students check out the association(s) at their school.

If no club exists, you may want to consider encouraging or helping your child start one. To start a Christian club, here are some things you need to find out:

- Does an adult have to sponsor the club? If so, a school staff person or parent may need to help run meetings and activities.
- Will a faculty member allow the club to use his or her room?
- Did a Christian club ever exist on the campus in the past, and if so, why does it no longer exist?
- How many Christians on campus are interested in a club? Rope some other potential leaders into the development process.
- What would other believers like from a club? Form a mission statement based on that information.
- Do other nearby schools have Christian clubs? If so, not only will you be able to learn from them, you may also be able to partner with them.
- What potential obstacles may arise? Brainstorm some ideas for how you might overcome problems that present themselves.
- Will your youth pastor help and support you? If so, in what ways?

Youth for Christ

Founded in 1944, Youth for Christ (YFC) started with rallies aimed at evangelizing students in local communities. In the late '50s and early '60s, YFC formed Bible clubs. According to the YFC Web site, the middle '60s and early '70s saw "Campus Life and Campus Life/JV ministries to senior and junior high youth [become] the thrust of YFC ministry."[1] Since then, Youth for Christ has developed several other ministries, including Youth Guidance (for at-risk and institutionalized youth), Teen Moms, and Urban Ministries.

Because of YFC's deep roots in evangelism, some families feel concerned that if students become too involved, they will miss out on important discipleship training. I completely understand this apprehension, but let me encourage potentially concerned parents in two ways.

First, YFC does more than just evangelize. The Campus Life and Campus Life/JV ministries seek to establish and encourage students as lifelong, passionate followers of Christ. Campus Life tries to help students make wise choices, positively impact their schools, and live out the gospel message. Campus Life meetings combine friendship with creative programs as well as opportunities for students to talk with others about their faith. This is a fabulous way for students to mature. If students can communicate their beliefs to peers or adults, they have begun to build a firm foundation in the Lord.

YFC leaders serve as role models of faith, hope, and love. The depth of their faith and the life-changing friendship they may build with your son or daughter can certainly provide more than opportunities for fun and outreach.

Second, Youth for Christ attempts not to replace the local church but assist it. If your son or daughter wants to attend only YFC meetings, try to help him or her understand that the goal of Youth for Christ is to build up the church, not take members away from it.

Campus Life may sponsor area events, trips, and activities that connect YFC students with those from other schools. This can be a great way to help your son or daughter experience both diversity and unity in the body of Christ.

Youth for Christ also offers summer-camp opportunities, designed to reach unchurched students and help Christians and non-Christians "fall deeper in love with God and His ways, through laughter, through tears, through renewed commitments, by repenting from sin, by forgiving one another, and by the silent recognition of the Maker of the mountains."[2]

In addition, YFC expanded its ministry twenty-eight years ago to include Project Serve, which provides missions experiences for groups and individuals. If your son or daughter is past eighth grade, you may want to consider this great opportunity to serve.

More recently, YFC began holding DC/LA Student Evangelism SuperConferences every three years. The purpose of these conferences (one in Washington DC, and one in Los Angeles) is to challenge and equip Christian students to impact their schools for Christ. This could be a fabulous chance for your son or daughter to grow in sharing the gospel and changing the world.

Fellowship of Christian Athletes

Since 1954 the Fellowship of Christian Athletes (FCA) has trained junior- and senior-high (as well as college and professional) athletes and coaches to impact their schools and their world for Christ.

FCA Huddles meet weekly on campuses or in homes. The purpose of Huddles is to make real FCA's core values to foster relationships that will "demonstrate steadfast commitments to Jesus Christ and His Word through integrity, serving, teamwork and excellence."[3]

FCA also sponsors sports and leadership camps, which intensely challenge students both physically and spiritually. In addition to the Huddle and camp ministries, FCA helps students say no to drugs and alcohol through the One Way 2 Play—Drug Free! program.

To find out if a Huddle exists on your son's or daughter's campus, how to start a huddle, or about the other FCA ministries, see the appendix at the back of this book.

Student Venture

Student Venture, the junior- and senior-high ministry of Campus Crusade for Christ, started in 1966. With more than thirteen hundred full-time staff, affiliates, and local community volunteers, Student Venture partners with sixty other organizations in developing campus movements designed to help students know and grow in Christ.[4]

The Win-Build-Send philosophy, which emphasizes winning people to Christ, helping them develop a solid faith, and sending them out to win others, seeks to meet young people "right where they are," and can minister to students at all levels of spiritual maturity.

I've had the privilege of knowing Student Venture national director Chuck Klein and can attest personally that his heartbeat for young people trickles down to many of the staff and students involved in Student Venture.

Young Life

In 1941 Young Life began making an impact on students' lives. In the sixty-plus years since, the organization has expanded to include both junior- and senior-high clubs, an amazing camp ministry, and now multicultural and urban outreaches.

The fourfold purpose of Young Life can be summed up as introducing, encouraging, providing, and helping.[5] Young Life facilitates encounters with Christ so that students might know Him. It also offers ways for students to grow in relationship with Jesus, sets students up with positive role models to spur them on in the Lord, and assists young people in gaining the skills, assets, and attitudes which will best prepare them for the future.

Young Life and "fun" seem to be synonymous. Club programs sponsor weekly gatherings packed with creativity, spontaneity, and a gospel message. These clubs may meet in someone's home, at a gym or neighborhood center, or at a church.

For those who wish to go deeper spiritually, Young Life provides weekly small groups as well as clubs. Called Campaigners, these Bible studies focus on examining the Word, praying, and applying biblical principles to life.

And then there are Young Life's amazing camps. Last year, both weekend and week-long camps gave more than ninety thousand students the opportunity to start and/or mature in their walk with Christ. One of my best friends, Brian Aaby, came to know the Lord at a Young Life camp and now works as a youth pastor, so I am all for these camps.

You should be aware that some Young Life camps register unchurched students first, so do not be discouraged if your son or daughter does not get to go. The spot he or she wanted to take may be filled by someone like Brian who will encounter the Lord and go on to serve Him for the rest of his or her life.

Young Life also had a huge impact on my life. My Young Life leader, Ted Montoya, became the youth pastor at my home church. He was the man God later used to call me into youth ministry.

Partnership, Not Competition

Parachurch ministries see themselves not as competing with local churches but in partnership with them. Young Life's Web site proclaims that "teens are encouraged to be part of a local church community, and Young Life partners with churches and parishes who share our vision to reach every [student]."[6]

Likewise, Youth for Christ declares that their "mission…is to participate in the body of Christ in responsible evangelism of youth...and discipling them into the local church."[7] Student Venture and FCA do not view their work as a way to replace the church, but rather as a way to build it. Christian clubs will not meet a student's every need, but they can certainly add to what training students receive elsewhere.

I present these ministries to you because I know that not every student will be able to—or want to—attend church functions. Times or days may not mesh with practices, concerts, or family activities. Your son or daughter may simply enjoy a parachurch Bible study more than a small group at church. Participating in any of the organizations I discussed can give your child other opportunities to grow in Christlikeness.

Encourage your son or daughter to find the places he or she fits best—whether in a club, an FCA Huddle, or a Young Life Campaigners Bible study. But exhort your child to also stay connected to the church as both servant and worshiper.

Youth Missions

Parents have often approached me to ask about mission opportunities outside the church. Perhaps their son or daughter has connected with an organization like Youth for Christ that sponsors its own mission trips. Maybe the dates of a youth ministry's outreach conflict with other family activities. Whatever the case, I heartily encourage parents to send their child on a mission trip to serve the Lord if he or she wants to go. A mission trip may shape and bless your son or daughter beyond measure, and I would hate to see a student miss out on the chance to reach outside his or her comfort zone.

I cannot list each of the reputable mission agencies here, especially since I have not worked with all of them. I would not want to lead a family in the wrong direction. I can say, however, that with a bit of research and a lot of prayer, God will direct you to the right project and organization.

Last summer a family I'd worked with for some years asked me about a mission trip their sixteen-year-old son was considering. The mother gave me some information, and I did a little additional homework, only to find out that the agency had some potential "issues."

I counseled the mom to look into these things herself, pray about the trip, and make a decision based on the Lord's leading and the knowledge she'd received. Ultimately, her son did not go on that trip but served on a different outreach later.

As long as the mission agency's doctrine is sound, you may consider any trip with that organization. However, some outreaches are not right for certain people. If your child has asthma, you may not want to send him or her to a high-altitude location. If a student struggles getting along with little kids, a VBS program may not be a great fit.

I think you get the point. Look for an agency that has an outstanding track record, a solid list of supporters, and a strong missionary base. An outreach that turns a student off to missions is worse than no youth mission experience at all.

OUTSIDE THE BOX, INSIDE THE FAMILY OF GOD

As you can see, the options for student ministry vary greatly. You do not have to feel stuck with one approach or even inside the walls of the church you attend. Within the body of Christ, your child may grow and mature in a multitude of places and programs. Help your son or daughter see that although a ministry may be outside the box of a traditional youth group, it can still be right inside the outstretched arms of the family of God.

What Parents Like You Had to Say

From Claire, mother of three daughters, all high-school graduates:

At the church we attended for some time, the youth ministry was made up of students from many high schools. The representation from my daughters' campus, however, was somewhat small. My girls enjoyed Student Venture tremendously, in part because it allowed them to connect with students from their own high school. They were also in Bible studies with girls from their classes. SV Leaders, some single and some married, would attend the girls' sporting events and other activities. Our daughters had awesome opportunities to grow in Student Venture as well. The sky was the limit! They were trained in missions, in speaking, in leading small groups, and in worship. The girls could invite friends to SV and everyone could participate at the level with which they felt comfortable and able. If they had wanted to, they could have simply attended large-group meetings now and then. But my girls went way beyond that. They each got involved with all kinds of studies, programs, and activities. Our family's association with Student Venture has been simply outstanding!

From Keith, father of two teenage sons and a daughter:

My wife and I believe that character development is the most significant aspect of education. My original motivation to homeschool was my belief that my wife and I could do a

better job of educating our children than our particular
public-school district had been doing up until that time. As
we continued to bring our younger children up in the homeschooling environment and grew more in our understanding
of the biblical mandate to train our children in the Lord, we
began to realize the spiritual, pragmatic, and intellectual truth
of God's Word, which teaches that if we train and instruct our
children to build godly character first, then the other things
we desire for them—intellectual, physical, and emotional
learning—will naturally and more easily follow. We truly
believe that, as Scripture teaches, if we seek first the kingdom
of God for our kids, all things will be added unto them (see
Matthew 6:33-34).

One of the godly life principles we want to instill in our
children is a devotion to service. We desire that they serve
within the church, and we have tried to help them find where
they fit best according to the individual skills God has given
them. All of our children participate at some level with the
children's and youth-ministry programs at our church. Yet
they have also done some things that have fortified them spiritually outside the church walls. For instance, my son and his
friends found themselves frustrated when they were in a
church Bible-study group with other high-school students
who did not place the same priority on spiritual growth. It
seemed that these young men were more interested in having
a good time and getting out of the house than in strengthening their relationship with God. My son and a couple of other
young men now meet on Monday nights to study Scripture
together, hold one another accountable, and pray for and with

each other. The fathers of these students (myself included) used to participate in and/or lead this study, but after two years, when the dads' schedules kept them from coming, our sons kept things going on their own.

I firmly believe that the local church acts as an umbrella designed by God to encompass and facilitate a variety of means of worship and service for families, whether at church, in the community, or at home. I also believe that God has clearly given Christians a mandate to serve with, participate in, and worship with the body of Christ. I would not want my son to feel that what he does with his friends in small-group Bible study takes the place of that. His participation in worship outside of church complements and enriches, rather than competes with, what happens in the youth ministry.

I've heard some families espouse the idea that if a family allows their children to be involved with a youth group, they will be more "tainted" by the immaturity of their peers than they will be "painted" by the youth pastor or teachers. While I can understand this, I believe that God wants me to discern which youth-group activities, events, and situations my sons or daughter will be able handle without succumbing to the temptations that are inherent in every community, church, school, or social function. This is by far one of the most difficult and sensitive aspects of raising children. But however challenging it is to determine at what point in your child's life it is appropriate to allow him or her to participate without a parent's direct supervision, I believe that a biblically sound church provides the best and safest opportunities outside the home to assist parents in teaching children to learn to serve

God, fellow believers, and their community in a Christlike capacity. Church is also the best and safest place to further our children's spiritual education. Our church's youth-ministry program has provided us with many opportunities to complement our children's spiritual maturity and development.

Ten

Transitioning Out of Youth Ministry

SOME OF YOU ARE years from even thinking about your child graduating from high school. Others of you have already begun filling out college applications or shedding tears as you think about your son or daughter making the huge transitions that happen post–high school.

As a youth minister I've graduated many students into the adventure of young adulthood. A great number of those I've shepherded chose to attend college, but many have made decisions to join the military, work full time, or enroll in a trade-school program.

No matter where my students go after high school, I ask God to keep their faith strong and their love for Him deep and thriving through the years following graduation. Sadly, however, statistics are against the fulfillment of this prayer.

In 2000 the Barna Research Group reported that "more than seven out of ten teens are engaged in some church-related effort in a typical week.... When asked to estimate the likelihood that they will continue to participate in church life once they are living on their own, levels dip precipitously, to only about one out of every three teens."

The Barna report goes on to say, "Placed in context, that stands as the lowest level of expected participation among teens recorded by Barna Research in more than a decade."[1]

As you may have noticed, this is only "expected participation." High-school ministries like Student Venture report that approximately 70 percent of students who claimed faith their senior year of high school stop attending church when they begin college.

As a parent I have to confess that these statistics terrify me. I hate to imagine my precious daughters, whom I've prayed for and loved in the Lord, heading off into adulthood and ditching church or, worse, ditching Christ. It kills me.

It also breaks my heart as a youth minister to think of the many students I've pastored who will become part of that 70 percent.

I believe that it's time for youth ministers and parents to partner in transitioning students from a childlike faith to an adult one. It's time we assist one another in keeping students faithful to Christ.

But how can we do this?

One step my ministry has taken is collaborating with a group in San Diego called Hand Off Ministry. I'd like to share with you the story of the ministry's founder, Robert Bekins. He writes:

When I went to the University of Colorado in 1965, my parents were moving from a final Marine Corps posting as a recruiter in Kansas City to retirement in Fallbrook, California. With 18 years of training in the...church and significant activities in youth [group] and the church choir, I should have been just fine. It didn't work out that way. In Boulder, I went to church twice [in four years] and never felt connected. I fell through the cracks and became lost. I would stay that way for more than twenty-five years [after college]. During that time, I hurt a lot of people, myself included. It grieves me to think of those days and [I] wish I could go back and undo [things].

When my son decided to go away to college in 2002, I determined that I was not going to let that fate fall to him as well....

He had also chosen Colorado, so for me the stakes were ele-
vated.... For weeks before his departure, I corresponded unilater-
ally with [a church] where he was headed.... They never returned
any calls or emails. I decided to drive him to Boulder [but] when
we got there, I had just one day before my turn around trip. We
found where [one church] was meeting...[but] a note on the door
explain[ed] that they were leaving town....

The next day, a weekday, I had to leave first thing in the
morning, without any resolution to my fears. [Yet] two weeks later,
a wonderful thing happened to my son. His dormitory Resident
Advisor invited him to his place of worship. My son found a new
church home and a band of Christian brothers and sisters with
whom to walk.[2]

Robert Bekins feels that what made the difference for his son was *personal contact* with another believer. Someone with whom he could attend
church. Someone with whom he could talk about life *and* matters of faith.
An older Christian with whom to place the craziness of college life in eternal context.

Because of his own painful past experience and his son's better one,
Bekins determined to start a ministry for families that would help stu-
dents transition from high-school to college ministry. And so, Hand Off
Ministry was born.

The goals of Hand Off are to "provide parents of...high school
graduates a list of churches, [near their son's or daughter's college],
from which they can choose. Having chosen, [Hand Off] will
contact pastors at the 'receiving church' and explain the program
to them. They will go to their congregation and seek a volunteer to
mentor the incoming student. We will contact the volunteer and
the student and put them in touch so that correspondence may

begin [before a student settles on campus]. When the student
arrives [at school], their mentor will help with a variety of things
like…transportation to the college [and] showing them where off-
campus libraries, malls, post offices, and pizza places may be
found. They will answer questions about the community. Most
importantly, they will transport them to church on Sunday and
help get them get connected to a college-level group within the
church." (For Hand Off Ministries contact information see the
resources section.)[3]

Sounds great, you may be thinking, *but what if Hand Off can't meet
my son's or daughter's needs?*

Don't worry. There are *many* such ministries operating around the
nation. This chapter will highlight some of the major ones, providing
descriptions as well as contact information that will help you connect your
son or daughter with a church and possibly an on-campus parachurch
organization. (Contact information for each of the ministries highlighted
in the chapter can be found in the appendix at the end of this book.)

But first let's look briefly at why it's difficult to help students transition out of youth ministry, what is actually happening on college campuses, and what practical advice the Bible gives us for sending off those
we love.

BELIEVE ME, I UNDERSTAND

Helping your child transition into an adult faith is *not* easy. I understand
because I am "in the business" with you.

Not only are students extremely busy their senior year and as they
graduate, but they also begin to distance themselves from parents and
other authorities (including pastors like me). They want to spread their
wings and assert their independence. They want to be free. But what they

may not realize is that with the freedoms of adulthood come a whole lot of responsibilities as well.

Today's college campuses are extraordinarily "free," at least by the world's standards of freedom. The trends of coed dormitories and even coed bathrooms have spread across the nation. The incidences of drug, alcohol, and nicotine abuse as well as sexual and verbal assault are off the charts already, and they're still rising.

When students leave high school, temptations and uncertainties seem to multiply. Yet this is often when many young people stop attending church. I believe that this is no less than the work of the Evil One, who would like nothing better than to draw young people away from the Lord just when they need Him most.

Listen the words of one college student:

> I've gone to church my whole life, and my spirituality has always been an influence in my life. As I went away to college, I didn't consider my faith in Christ an important part of who I was, and consequently, I didn't care that I was continuing to turn my back on God. I turned to my friends in my dorm to find my identity and got into drinking, drugs, and sexual immorality.[4]

Dr. James Dobson, founder of Focus on the Family, has said, "I doubt if...parents realize just how antagonistic...colleges have become to anything that smacks of Christianity.... The Christian perspective is not only excluded from the classroom, it is often ridiculed and undermined."

I suppose we shouldn't be too surprised by this. Peter recognized centuries ago that "[our] enemy the devil prowls around like a roaring lion looking for someone to devour" (1 Peter 5:8).

What better way for the Adversary to attack the young people of today than to "get them" as they make one of the most challenging transitions in life? Many students, including those who do not choose to attend college, leave home after high-school graduation. They are on their own for the first time, and the Enemy knows that if he can turn them from the truth, he may have them for the remainder of their lives.

The Bible gives us a great model for sending a student off into the world. In Acts 20:17-38, Paul addressed the elders in Ephesus for the last time. He did four things to prepare them for the times of temptation and trial ahead. These biblical principles help us understand how we can work with our children before and as they transition out of youth ministry.

In his article "Helping Seniors Finish Strong," Ben Burns describes four principles Acts 20 teaches youth workers to follow when working with young people: reminisce, encourage, caution, and launch.[5] In my own adaptation of his material, I want to encourage parents to apply these same principles with their children:

1. *Reminisce.* Just as the apostle Paul *blessed* the Ephesians, I encourage you to bless your child before she leaves home. Tell her how much you love her and enjoy spending time with her. Share some of the great memories you have of the times you've spent together. Highlight how you've seen her grow spiritually. Emphasize that you believe God has a loving plan specifically for her.

2. *Encourage.* Paul exhorted the Ephesians to "keep watch over" themselves (Acts 20:28). You need to encourage your child to do the same. Share with him that God wants to use him wherever he is. Encourage him to serve, perhaps as a Bible-study leader or in some other way. Exhort him to share his faith with others. Help him see that God wants him to be part of His amazing work on earth.

3. *Caution.* Paul told the Ephesians that they would face great spiritual challenges after he left them, and he encouraged them to be on their guard (see Acts 20:29-31). Walk your child through the temptations that may arise after high

school. Arm her with biblical reasons to abstain from substance abuse, promiscuity, and other destructive habits. Encourage her to go against the grain and to stand out for Christ. Tell her that when she feels lonely, stressed (from academic or interpersonal pressures), or persecuted by others who mock God's Word, she can call you. Assure her that these feelings are normal and that the Lord will help her overcome.

4. *Launch.* Paul did not hold on to the Ephesians. Instead, he let them go, entrusting them into God's hands to do the work He wanted them to do (see Acts 20:32). Paul took the risk that those he loved might walk away from God because he knew they would not be able to grow if he held on. You, too, need to release your child. Rest in the peace that the almighty God will walk beside and before your child and that no matter what mistakes her or she may make, God "who began a good work in [him or her] will carry it on to completion until the day of Christ Jesus" (Philippians 1:6).

Life after high school may seem like a scary season to us, but God is as present on every campus and in every workplace in the nation as He is in every church. You can trust your son or daughter to Him.

You Can Also…

While trusting God is the first step in helping your child transition into adulthood, if you're like me, you usually want to do something more "active" next. And you and I can't invest our energy in anything better than praying for the students heading into adulthood.

I'd like to help you develop a strategy for praying over your graduating or graduated child.[6] Following are a few suggestions to get you started. Add to and personalize this list to best suit your son's or daughter's needs:

- Pray that God will enable your child (with your help) to make wise decisions, such as whether or not to attend college, and if so, which one, how far away, what major, etc.
- Pray specifically for your child's spiritual development during the years after he or she graduates from high school. Pray for mentors, friends, the right classes or job, a church, a godly working environment, and other details of life, including wise stewardship, the development of adult interpersonal skills, and sensible time management. You can even pray that he won't live on french fries, ramen noodles, and Oreos during this time.
- If your child isn't attending college, pray that he or she might consider a postgraduation ministry opportunity. Organizations such as Youth with a Mission (YWAM), Navigators, and others offer positions for students just out of high school. A one- to two-year stint like this can really solidify and mature a teen's faith.

If your child does decide to attend college...

- Look into and, if possible, try to visit the Christian fellowships on campus as well as area churches. Pray for those ministries and for godly connections with all students, not just your son or daughter. Ask God to help your child find the right church.
- Visit the college your son or daughter chooses so that when he or she mentions this place or that, you'll recognize the names and be able to pray specifically for events, classes, and even dorms.
- Pray that your son or daughter will connect with at least one Christian professor.
- Pray that your teen will be "adopted" by a family in a new church.
- Pray for the right roommate.

I've observed several reasons why students abandon their faith. Among the most prominent are (1) lingering doubts about God, the church, and the Bible; (2) other activities or relationships—school, friendships, dating, sports—that displace faith as a priority in a student's life; (3) a relationship with God that doesn't seem to be "paying off"; and (4) a tendency to rely on the faith of family, church leaders, or friends rather than investing personally in Christ.

Pray through each of these factors, asking God to answer your child's questions and bring others into his or her life to help process the doubts and concerns that *will* arise as he or she becomes an adult. Pray that the Lord would allow your child to see that although life (and faith) doesn't always work as *we* plan, nothing happens that God does not know about and use. Pray that the Lord would not permit anything to become more significant than love for and worship of Him. And pray, above all, that your child would develop his or her own walk with Christ.

Of course, these are only a few of the things you can pray for your graduating or graduated teen. I'm confident that as you pray, God will uniquely guide your intercession, enabling you to lift your son or daughter up in the right ways.

(*Note:* If your son or daughter chooses not to attend college, you may want to skip to the "Totally Off-Campus" section, since the following pages deal with collegiate issues.)

BEFORE THEY GRADUATE

There are also a number of excellent college preparatory seminars and courses in which you and/or your child can participate before high-school graduation.

CollegeWalk, a ministry of Campus Crusade for Christ, puts on College Prep Seminars that train pastors, small-group leaders, and parents to prepare students to deal with the challenges and temptations they will face in college.

You can partner with your youth pastor to sponsor a seminar like this at your church or get a group of parents together and host your own seminar. But be aware that there are costs involved. CollegeWalk recommends charging those who attend the program to cover expenses.

While the seminar works best for second-semester high-school juniors (the course also includes a section on choosing the right college), it could certainly be beneficial for younger students and even for first-semester high-school seniors, many of whom have not yet selected a college.

By the way, this seminar is geared toward students who have determined that they want to attend college, so if your son or daughter is not interested in college, this seminar is probably not right for your child.

Another program I highly recommend is Summit Ministries. One of the main reasons I recommend this ministry is because so many young people tend to fall away from Christ during the post-high-school years when their faith is tested by friends, professors, or colleagues who espouse other worldviews.

Dr. James Dobson sent his son Ryan through the Summit program and has since featured the ministry on Focus on the Family's nationally and internationally syndicated radio broadcast.

Summit's promotional material describes the ministry as follows:

[Summit is] an educational Christian ministry whose very existence is a response to our current post-Christian culture. Countless Christians, and especially Christian youth, are renouncing their faith and countless more are adopting the false humanistic philosophies of our day.

Summit views its role in God's kingdom as a catalyst to counteract this alarming trend. However, our ultimate goal [supersedes] simply training. As Christians are challenged to stand strong in their faith and defend truth, they will also be equipped to have a positive influence on the society in which they live.

David A. Noebel, founder and president of Summit Ministries, almost joined the statistics [and fell away from Christ], when he was a philosophy student at the University of Wisconsin in Madison. Dr. Noebel founded Summit in 1962 to help ground Christians in their faith, thereby enabling them to face the barrage of challenges whirling about on college campuses.[7]

Currently Summit hosts eight two-week conferences every summer, all at their home base in Manitou Springs, Colorado. At the foot of Pikes Peak, Summit Village enjoys not only breathtaking views but fabulous access to outdoor recreational activities as well, many of which are available at no cost for Summit students.

A spring conference, held once a year at the Navigators' Glen Eyrie Castle, equips students in much the same manner as the summer conferences do. Because of the shorter time frame, however, this spring week is a bit more intense.

Summit takes students as young as sixteen, but since the ministry focus is on preparation for college and the issues students will face there, it might be best for students to attend a conference after their junior or senior year of high school.

The ministry also offers weekend programs for families and pastors. In addition, individuals, families, churches, Sunday schools, homeschools, or Christian schools can purchase curriculum materials from Summit. What great opportunities Summit Ministries provides for families, small groups, or an entire church to grow stronger in faith and in knowledge of Christ!

Not only have several of my youth-group students graduated from the Summit program, but I have also used the curriculum for my high-school students and small groups. I enthusiastically recommend Summit's materials and conferences. Like the CollegeWalk College Prep Seminars, Summit Ministries charges for conferences and programs. But believe me when I say that it is well worth your investment.

I've recently become aware of another program that I also highly recommend. Connected with Biola University, an excellent Christian college in Southern California, the STAR Torrey Academy wants to develop "whole souls: minds that think, hearts with a passion for the Good and hands that act in the world."[8]

As their Web site claims,

Because the world is in need of winsome, thoughtful, intellectual Christians, STAR Torrey Academy is committed to cultivating the spiritual and intellectual integrity of each student through the education of the whole soul.

STAR Torrey Academy seeks to provide an environment in which students can wrestle with issues of faith and intellect through respectful dialogue while learning to identify and critique philosophies in light of the Bible. Students are trained to read great literature, identify the philosophies embedded therein, and analyze the impact of those writings upon their contemporaries and generations following.

While using the Socratic method to teach students *how* to think, not *what* to think, STAR Torrey Academy upholds the Bible as the word of God, maintains the centrality of Christ, and challenges students to impact their generation for the Lord Jesus Christ.[9]

After reading this description, you may assume that only "smart" kids should attend Torrey Academy. This is absolutely not the case. Students of all academic levels have thrived at Torrey. Those with a variety of learning disabilities have also successfully completed the program.

Torrey offers semester-long classes for sophomore, junior, and senior students. Those within the state of California can take classes at Biola University or at several off-campus locations, including Garden Grove, South Orange County, Yorba Linda, Fresno, Reseda, San Dimas, Santa

Barbara, Temecula, Thousand Oaks, and Visalia. For those living outside California, Torrey offers online opportunities during homeschool hours as well as in the evening.

OTHER HELPS

The CollegeWalk Web site states, "We desire that Christian students get involved in a ministry on their campus that will provide them with the environment that encourages spiritual growth and involvement." The site goes on to say that sometimes students "just need someone to help [them] find an environment where [they] can continue to grow spiritually."[10]

To that end, CollegeWalk partners with Campus Alliance (an association coordinated by the National Network of Youth ministries) and nine national collegiate ministries to provide students with information about parachurch organizations at and around specific colleges. It also offers students the opportunity to share with individual ministries limited personal information, such as their name, address, e-mail, and the college they plan to attend. This allows ministries to contact students before they ever set foot on campus.

CollegeWalk also helps students find the right church by offering an excellent article titled "Choosing a Church" that students can download for free from the ministry Web site.[11] Based upon the ideas in this article, I've developed several important guidelines for students to consider when searching for a dynamic church:

- Participation in church is not an option. God calls us to live in community for our own good and for the good of others. Keeping this in mind, choose a church that you can commit to attending *regularly.*
- Fellowship with other believers is essential. Look for a place you can mingle with people who are *not* at your same age and stage.

This will help connect you with older believers who might encourage you in your faith as well as less mature Christians whom you might build up.

- Consider the church leadership. Find out about the pastors and elders. Are they living lives that you would like to imitate? (See Hebrews 13:7.)
- Look for your ministry niche. Church is not merely about what you can *get,* but about how you can *give.* Look for a place where you can serve others.
- Check the church's doctrine. Read the statement of faith and any literature the church provides about its programs and views. Are worship, prayer, praise, the Bible, and missions prioritized at this church?
- Find a church that's the right size. During the college years students can easily get lost in the vacuum between high-school and adult ministries. Find a church that's either small enough for you to be known or large enough to have a thriving college and career ministry.

The CollegeWalk maintains another Web site that is devoted to helping students locate a church.[12] There you will find links to the Power to Change database of partnering churches, the Willow Creek Association church-finder service, and the *Gospelcom.org* database of churches. Because some church-finder services only include listings, not statements of faith, it's always best to contact directly the churches in which you might be interested.

The CollegeWalk site also has a *Resources* link that lists several helpful books, including *How to Stay Christian in College* and *Navigating the Road Ahead.* Also listed are the *Essential College Kit from Family Life* and the *BreakPoint College Survival Kit.* Both include literature that helps students prepare to live as Christians while at college.

The Fellowship of Christian Athletes (FCA) has teamed up (as CollegeWalk has) with a number of Christian colleges in an effort to provide parents and students with information that will help them make college decisions. The FCA Web site includes a *Free College Info* link that allows students to view the profiles of a select number of Christian colleges. Students may then request free information by linking to the schools that interest them.

ON-CAMPUS MINISTRIES

Connecting your child with an on-campus ministry may also help him or her stay focused on a relationship with Christ and fellowship with other believers. There are a number of collegiate ministries from which to choose, depending on the school your son or daughter decides to attend. Some universities have their own on-campus ministries, and some colleges have representatives from national ministries who run a campus-wide branch of their organization. Some schools have both.

Most campus ministries fall under the category of "parachurch organizations." As I mentioned earlier, this simply means that college ministries like the ones I will describe on the following pages do not seek to replace the church, but rather to partner with it.

While you read, keep in mind that it's best to familiarize yourself with the particular ministries available at the college your child has selected. I've also included some descriptions of the larger national ministries. Contact information for each of these ministries can be found in the appendix of this book.

The Navigators

The Navigators' Collegiate Ministry believes in one-to-one, life-to-life interaction between students and more mature believers. Mentoring and discipleship form the foundation for the Navigators' ministry.

Navs helps students learn the basic tenets of the Christian faith as well as how to study the Bible and apply it to daily life. In addition, Navigators staff members coach college students in communicating their faith, balancing their priorities, and developing their character.

The Navigators also holds large-group meetings and events to promote unity and fellowship. These times focus on fun as well as spiritual formation. Throughout the semester, Navs may host conferences, retreats, and summer-long opportunities.

InterVarsity Christian Fellowship (ICF)

The purpose and commitment statements of InterVarsity Christian Fellowship affirm,

> In response to God's love, grace and truth: The Purpose of Inter-
> Varsity Christian Fellowship/USA is to establish and advance at
> colleges and universities witnessing communities of students and
> faculty who follow Jesus Christ as Savior and Lord: growing in love
> for God, God's Word, God's people of every ethnicity and culture,
> and God's purposes in the world.
>
> We are called to be a redeeming influence among [a college's]
> people, ideas and structures.[13]

To achieve the goals they have set, InterVarsity staff members serve on 565 college campuses in the United States.

InterVarsity ministries on different campuses run distinct programs suited to the specific needs and makeup of the college or university with which they partner. The common denominator for all InterVarsity fellowships, however, is love for Jesus Christ and commitment to train others who will then reach the world for Christ.

InterVarsity also formed specialized areas of ministry some time ago. Some schools have separate chapters for international students who are studying in the United States as well as for sororities and fraternities. African American Student Fellowships, Asian American Student Fellowships, and Latino Fellowships can be found on campuses throughout the nation.

Campus Crusade for Christ

In 1951, founders Bill and Vonette Bright launched Campus Crusade to "win the campus today and change the world tomorrow."[14] Today, CCC is the largest collegiate ministry in the United States, with 1,029 campuses staffed and equipped to "serve as a spiritual resource to students, providing information, training, relationships, opportunities and environments that are conducive to spiritual growth."[15]

Campus Crusade staff members meet with students to answer questions, help them grow spiritually, and assist them in developing their own ministries. Typically a large meeting is held once a week to unite everyone involved and to offer opportunities to attract prebelievers. The meeting can include drama, music, and a speaker. Campus Crusade also sponsors outreach activities on campus to help students understand what it means to have a personal relationship with Christ.

CCC also recognizes that "as more and more ethnic students come to campus, they are increasingly immersing themselves in an ethnic student subculture."[16] To reach these groups, Campus Crusade formed Ethnic Student Ministries (ESM). With sixty-four ESM movements spread throughout the United States in Destino (for Hispanic and Latino students), Epic (for Asian American students), and Impact (for African American students) groups, Campus Crusade reaches many students who may not feel comfortable in other ministries.

Smaller Ministries

In addition to introducing you to the larger campus ministries, I'd like to alert you to three smaller ministries (all Web site information is in the appendix):

- Baptist students could check out Baptist Student Unions sponsored on U.S. campuses.
- The Wesley Foundation helps Methodist students connect with Wesleyan ministries, particularly those geared to students interested in professional ministry or church-related higher education.
- The Evangelical Free Church also has on-campus ministries connecting college students with one another.

Totally Off-Campus

Some students who choose not to pursue post-high-school education may still attend the college group at their church, but many feel out of place when pastors or leaders talk about things like schoolwork and campus events.

Sadly, in many churches a major vacuum exists between high-school and young-family ministries. I say this not to discourage parents of professional or working high-school graduates, but to prepare you for the different kind of transition you can help your son or daughter face.

After helping your child develop a personal passion for Christ, your primary responsibility can be helping him or her become a fulfilled member and an active contributor in the church. If possible, connect your son or daughter with a mentor and a ministry for college-age adults *before* high-school graduation. Assist your child in finding where to "fit" within the body of Christ. Those who serve and feel part of a church will be less likely to abandon their faith after high school.

Don't worry if your child wishes to attend a different church than the one in which he or she was raised. If the service at which your son or daughter desires to worship is biblically sound and focused on God's glory, give him or her the freedom to express adult faith. Forcing your child to stay at your church while in your home may backfire, causing your son or daughter to resent rather than relish his or her first church experiences as an adult.

Those who choose not to attend college may grow up more quickly than their friends on campus. Working a forty-hour-per-week job or attending a professional school to prepare for entering the work force as soon as possible definitely pushes a young person toward adulthood.

Let your child become an independent, adult Christian and person. This can be a real challenge for graduated students living at home. Learning to set appropriate boundaries with parents and making their own choices may be entirely new experiences for them.

Here are just a few ways that you can direct and encourage your child without trying to control things:

- Give her space, privacy, and time to figure out her adult life.
- Dialogue with him about what he is experiencing without trying to tell him what to do and when. (Obviously, if he is endangering you, your family, or your home, you need to establish some boundaries.)
- Allow her to fail if need be. The Lord often works through our failings even more powerfully than through our successes.
- Most important, provide a consistent example for your young adult of what it means to be responsible and growing in relationship with Jesus.

PLANS TO PROSPER, NOT TO HARM

This chapter may have seemed a bit overwhelming to you. Don't worry; you're not crazy to feel that way! Guiding your son or daughter in the post-high-school years—when he or she is developing an adult faith—can be difficult. But the fruit of faithfully helping your son or daughter transition out of youth ministry will be well worth the efforts you must make.

Allow me to close this chapter with some final encouragement to those whose children walk away from their faith after high school: God will never allow your son or daughter to go farther than His reach. He *will* complete His good work in your child, and He *can* orchestrate situations designed to draw your son or daughter back to Himself. While the ultimate choice to follow Jesus is up to individuals, God *will* call to them throughout their whole life.

In *Why Christian Kids Leave the Faith,* Tom Bisset notes that 85 percent of religious dropouts return to the faith and values of their youth by the time they are twenty-four years old.[17] Bisset encourages parents to keep the lines of communication—and more important, the channels of love—open during the postgraduation years, no matter what choices a child makes. Show interest in your son's or daughter's life and ideas even if you disagree with his or her choices.

You could help your child see why you have chosen faith rather than other things that supposedly bring fulfillment. But you can only do this *if* you can guide your child without pushing him or her farther from Christ. "Tough love" requires tremendous wisdom, discernment, and grace.

Model as consistently as you can what it means to be a Christian, extending God's unconditional love to your child whenever possible. Place your trust in God, who has plans to prosper and not to harm, plans to give His children hope and a future (see Jeremiah 29:11).

Whether you are sending your child into the world, launching him or her into a college experience, or walking with your child through the fire of rebellion after he or she leaves youth ministry, "Trust in the LORD with all your heart and lean not on your own understanding; in all your ways acknowledge him, and he will make your paths straight" (Proverbs 3:5-6).

What Parents Like You Had to Say

From Joel and Laura, parents of three grown children:

When our children entered the teenage years, we felt it was crucial to stay as connected with them as we could. We tried to evaluate which areas of faith they seemed strongest in and which areas might need some work. Knowing the temptations and challenges they would face in the years after high school, we did all we could to prepare them for adulthood. We focused on encouraging their strengths and shoring up their weaknesses.

As it became clear that our eldest would leave home to attend college, we began giving him greater freedom, but always within limits. We had observed some Christian teens who arrived at the university and overindulged their newfound freedoms. So we decided to help our son experience a higher degree of freedom *at home,* before he had it at school. We did this with our other two as well. Of course there were risks in holding on "loosely" to our maturing children, but we genuinely wanted them to discover God's best in a personal way. We longed for them to learn that *their own* relationship with God was reliable.

Throughout our son's college career, and after our daughter left for college, we stayed actively involved in their lives by phone, e-mail, and through prayer. Though our children would only say so much to us, we became skilled "decoders" of what lay beneath the surface of their words. I believe this allowed us to pray for our kids and love them more effectively.

Finally, we tried to make it clear to our children that they ultimately made the choice whether to live a godly life. When our son's college soccer team began engaging in unhealthy behaviors, he made the decision to follow the path of righteousness. Though she could have taken jobs elsewhere, our daughter chose to work at a Christian school where her life of faith could bless others. Of course, this is exactly what we hoped to see—our children leaving the home and making faith their own.

A Benediction

THANK YOU FOR journeying with me through the world of youth ministry. It's been quite a ride, and I hope you've enjoyed it as much as I did. Truly, this book has been a delight to write.

I am crazy about my job and genuinely love students and their families. This opportunity to speak into the lives of so many parents and guardians has been simply incredible. I am grateful for you and your commitment to understanding what happens after you drop your son and daughter off at church.

And let me also express my thanks for being interested in your child's church experience. These years are crucial for your son or daughter, and by reading this book, you have taken a great step toward maximizing your child's involvement in youth group.

I pray that you have been encouraged about the different ways you can partner with the youth ministry at your church, whether through volunteering, using your resources, praying, or in the best case scenario, all three!

At times you may have felt overwhelmed by the exhortations or suggestions in a particular chapter. Please don't feel discouraged. These guidelines and tips are intended as encouragements, not commands. You most likely won't be able to follow every suggestion all at once or even over the years your son or daughter attends youth group.

You can always revisit a chapter when the need arises. For instance, if you experience feelings of frustration, you can skim through chapter 7 ("Dealing with Disappointment"). If you are considering joining the youth ministry's volunteer staff, chapter 5 ("Partnering with a Youth Ministry") may help you make an informed decision. And when it's time for your child to say good-bye to youth ministry, the final chapter can help your entire family through the transition.

This book is a reference tool to which I hope you will return or to which you can refer other parents and family members.

I leave all of us parents with this blessing, this benediction from God's Word:

> And this is my prayer: that your love may abound more and more in knowledge and depth of insight, so that you may be able to discern what is best and may be pure and blameless until the day of Christ, filled with the fruit of righteousness that comes through Jesus Christ—to the glory and praise of God. (Philippians 1:9-11)

As we love more, as our relationship with Christ grows, and as we are made holy and righteous, we *will* know how to best train up our children in the way they should go (see Proverbs 22:6). What an awesome promise with which to end our journey together!

Resources

BAPTIST STUDENT MINISTRIES/BAPTIST STUDENT UNIONS
Contact the National Collegiate Ministry Network
www.ncmnetwork.com (This Web site includes a link to *www*
.student.org, which provides state-specific listings of Baptist Student
Ministries.)

CAMPUS CRUSADE FOR CHRIST
National Office
100 Lake Hart Drive
Orlando, FL 32832
407-826-2000
www.campuscrusadeforchrist.com

COLLEGEWALK
A ministry of Campus Crusade for Christ
100 Lake Hart Drive, Dept. 25-SL
Orlando, FL 32832
1-800-678-LINC
E-mail: collegewalk@uscm.org
www.collegewalk.com

EVANGELICAL FREE CHURCH OF AMERICA
National Office
901 East 78th Street
Minneapolis, MN 55420-1300
1-800-745-2202
www.efca.org

FELLOWSHIP OF CHRISTIAN ATHLETES
8701 Leeds Road
Kansas City, MO 64129
1-800-289-0909
E-mail: fca@fca.org
www.fca.org

HAND OFF MINISTRY
Attn: Robert N. Bekins
PO Box 231795
Encinitas, CA 92023-1795
760-944-8557
Fax: 760-044-8531
E-mail: bekind5@juno.com

INTERVARSITY CHRISTIAN FELLOWSHIP/USA
6400 Schroeder Road
PO Box 7895
Madison, WI 53707-7895
608-274-9001
Fax: 608-274-7882
E-mail: information@intervarsity.org
www.intervarsity.org

THE NAVIGATORS
PO Box 6000
Colorado Springs, CO 80934
719-598-1212
Fax: 719-260-0479
http://home.navigators.org/us/collegiate/index.cfm

STUDENT VENTURE
A Ministry of Campus Crusade for Christ
National Office
100 Lake Hart Drive, Dept. 3200
Orlando, FL 32832-0100
1-800-699-4678
www.studentventure.com

SUMMIT MINISTRIES
PO Box 207
Manitou Springs, CO 80829
719-685-9103
www.summit.org

TORREY ACADEMY
Biola University STAR Program
12625 La Mirada Blvd.
Suite 103
La Mirada, CA 90638
562-906-4534
www.biola.com/community/torrey_academy

UNDERSTANDING YOUR TEENAGER
PO Box 420
Lakeside, CA 92040
1-800-561-9309
www.uyt.com

WESLEY FOUNDATION
College Bound
c/o General Board of Higher Education and Ministry
PO Box 340007
1001 Nineteenth Avenue, South
Nashville, TN 37203-0007
www.gbhem.org/asp/campusmin.asp (This Web site includes links to or
    contact information for the campus ministries sponsored by the
    United Methodist Church.)

YOUNG LIFE
PO Box 520
Colorado Springs, CO 80901
719-381-1800
719-381-1867 (Multicultural and Urban Young Life Ministry)
www.younglife.org

YOUTH FOR CHRIST
PO Box 4478
Englewood, CO 80155
303-843-9000
Fax: 303-843-9002
www.yfc.net

Notes

Introduction

1. Dr. Richard Ross et al., "A Call to Youth Ministers and the Church About Parent Ministry" (forum, The National Network of Youth Ministries, Glorieta, New Mexico, January 11–12, 2004), www.youthspecialties.com/articles/topics/family/call_parent_ministry.php.
2. Ross et al., "A Call to Youth Ministers."

Chapter 1

1. John F. MacArthur, ed., *The MacArthur Student Bible* (Nashville: Word, 2000), 1644.
2. Doug Fields, *Purpose-Driven Youth Ministry* (Grand Rapids: Zondervan, 1998), 251.

Chapter 3

1. Carnegie Council, *Great Transitions: Preparing Adolescents for a New Century* (New York: Carnegie Corporation, 1996), 19.

Chapter 4

1. I am deeply indebted to Rick Warren for the creation of the SHAPE model, which has provided an outstanding framework for helping parents determine how best to support youth ministry.

Chapter 5

1. Michael Cromartie, "What American Teenagers Believe: A Conversation with Christian Smith," Books and Culture, January/February 2005, 10-11.

2. Cromartie, "What American Teenagers Believe," 10-11.
3. The application and cover letter I used have been adapted from those originally created by the staff at First Evangelical Free Church of Fullerton. Without the wisdom of Doug Haag and Eric Heard, as well as additions made by Barry Bandera, the present high-school pastor, I would not have been able to share this with you.
4. Youth Specialties publishes several excellent resources, including *Help! I'm a Small-Group Leader!* by Laurie Polich (Zondervan, 1998) and *Help! I'm a Volunteer Youth Worker!* by Doug Fields (Zondervan, 1993). These and other helpful resources can be purchased at *www.youthspecialties.com.*

Chapter 6

1. Richard Foster, *Celebration of Discipline: The Path to Spiritual Growth* (New York: Harper & Row, 1978), 30.
2. Foster, *Celebration of Discipline,* 31.
3. Foster, *Celebration of Discipline,* 33.
4. See Richard Foster, *Prayer: Finding the Heart's True Home* (San Francisco: HarperSanFrancisco, 1992), 119-127.
5. Sören Kierkegaard, *Christian Discourses,* trans. Walter Lowie (Oxford, UK: Oxford University Press, 1940), 324.
6. Foster, *Celebration of Discipline,* 30.
7. See Janet Holm McHenry, *Prayer Changes Teens: How to Parent from Your Knees* (New York: Random House, 2003), 3.

Chapter 7

1. See Duffy Robbins, *Youth Ministry Nuts & Bolts* (Grand Rapids: Zondervan, 1990), 237-240.

Chapter 8

1. For further information on constructive criticism, read *Constructive Feedback* by Roland and Frances Bee (London, England: Chartered Institute of Personnel and Development, 1998). This brief yet pointedly insightful book can be purchased online through *www.alibris.com*. Another helpful resource is *The Power of Positive Criticism* by Hendrie Weisinger (New York: AMACOM, 2000). You can find this book on *www.amazon.com*. As far as I know, neither Weisinger nor the Bees claim to be Christians. So be aware that the material presented in these books may not come from a faith-based perspective and should therefore be applied with biblical wisdom.

2. Jaime Walters, "The 4-1-1 on Constructive Criticism," *Ivy SeaZine*, August 2001, www.ivysea.compages/ct0801_1.html; also www.inc.com/articles/2001/08/23257.html.

Chapter 9

1. Information provided under the "Our Story" heading on the About Us page of the Youth for Christ Web site, http://community .gospelcom.net/Brix?pageID=6545.

2. 2004 Youth for Christ purpose statement for YFCamp program, http://community.gospelcom.net/Brix?pageID=6552.

3. 2004 Fellowship of Christian Athletes purpose statement for Huddles, www.fca.org/aboutfca.

4. Student Venture, information provided in About Us, www.student venture.com/aboutus/index.htm.

5. 2005 Young Life purpose statement, www.younglife.org/pages/ whatisyl.html

6. Young Life, information provided in About Young Life, www.younglife.org/pages/aboutYL.htm.

7. 2004 Youth for Christ mission statement, http://community .gospelcom.net/Brix?pageID=6987.

Chapter 10

1. Barna Research Group, "Teenagers Embrace Religion but Are Not Excited About Christianity," *The Barna Update,* January 10, 2000, www.barna.org. Accessed April 22, 2005.
2. Robert Bekins, promotional material for Hand Off Ministry.
3. Bekins, Hand Off Ministry.
4. The words of anonymous college student that originally appeared on the CollegeWalk Web site, www.collegewalk.com.
5. See Burns, "Helping Seniors Finish Strong," *Network Magazine,* March 2003, 3-4.
6. I am indebted to Susan Alexander Yates and her excellent work *And Then I Had Teenagers: Encouragement for Parents of Teens and Preteens* (Grand Rapids: Baker, 2001), which inspired my thinking on this subject and provided me with fresh ways of encouraging parents to pray for students.
7. Information provided on the About Summit and Our History pages of the Summit Ministries Web site, www.summit.org.
8. Dr. John Mark Reynolds, director of the Torrey Honors Institute and advisor for the STAR Torrey Academy, www.biola.com/ community/torrey_academy.
9. STAR Torrey Academy mission and vision statement, www.biola .com/community/torrey_academy/about.
10. Information provided on the About Us and index pages of the CollegeWalk Web site, www.collegewalk.com/about.htm; www.collegewalk.com/index.htm.
11. "Choosing a Church," 1999, http://growinginchrist.com/church article.pdf. Also found at www.collegewalk.com/locator.htm.

12. To access the church locator on the CollegeWalk Web site, go to www.collegewalk.com/churches.htm. This page provides links to Web-based locator services.

13. Purpose and commitment statements of InterVarsity Christian Fellowship, www.intervarsity.org/aboutus/purpose.php; www.intervarsity.org/aboutus/commitments.php.

14. Information provided on the About Us page of the Campus Crusade for Christ Web site, www.campuscrusadeforchrist.com/aboutus/index.htm.

15. Information provided on the Frequently Asked Questions page of the Campus Crusade for Christ Web site, www.campuscrusadeforchrist.com/aboutus/FAQs.htm#4.

16. Information provided on the Ethnic Student Ministries page of the Campus Crusade for Christ Web site, www.campuscrusadeforchrist.com/aboutus/esm.htm.

17. See Tom Bisset, *Why Christian Kids Leave the Faith* (Grand Rapids: Discovery House, 1992), 147.

About the Author

JERAMY CLARK (MDiv) serves as pastor of high-school ministries at Emmanuel Faith Community Church in California. Previously he worked with students from middle school through college at Tri-Lakes Chapel in Monument, Colorado, and with high-school students at the First Evangelical Free Church of Fullerton, California. More than fourteen years of youth-ministry experience have taught Jeramy invaluable lessons about working with families. He lives in Escondido, California, with his wife, Jerusha, and daughters Jocelyn and Jasmine. Together, Jeramy and Jerusha have written three books—*I Gave Dating a Chance; He's HOT, She's HOT;* and *Define the Relationship*—and they have also contributed to *Five Paths to Finding the Love of Your Life*.

Can't-miss advice on guy/girl relationships from best-selling authors Jeramy and Jerusha Clark.

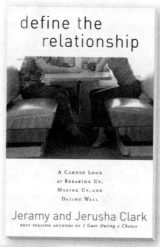

WATERBROOK PRESS
www.waterbrookpress.com